STAAR Prep
Grade 3
Reading Comprehension
Second Edition

by Mark Lyons

Item Code RAS 2581 • Copyright © 2013 Queue, Inc.

All rights reserved. No part of the material protected by this copyright may be reproduced or utilized in any form or by any means, electronic or mechanical, including photocopying, recording, or by any information storage and retrieval system. Printed in the United States of America.

Queue, Inc. • 80 Hathaway Drive, Stratford, CT 06615
(800) 232-2224 • Fax: (800) 775-2729 • www.qworkbooks.com

Table of Contents

Lucky 1

Annual Neighborhood Book Sale 5

Janet's Diary 9

The Bus Ride 13

What's for Dessert? 18

The Power of the Wind 23

They Fall From the Sky 30

He Found What Was Special 34

Silk Spinners 38

Maria's Idea 42

Beavers 47

My Life as a Colonist 51

Which Plant Will Grow the Tallest? 55

The Big Brother 61

The Bake Sale 66

Lazy Dog 71

Benjamin Franklin's Journal 75

The Wind 80

Someone to Count On 84

Problem Solved 89

The Tallest Animal 94

Read the story "Lucky" before answering the questions below.

My Notes About What I Am Reading

LUCKY

1. "I have to get to the ball fields for the baseball tryouts!" Ben said to his grandfather. Ben rushed out the front door and hopped onto his bike. He pedaled rapidly down the alley behind his grandfather's house. "I'll see you tomorrow," Ben called over his shoulder

2. Ben glanced at his watch. He had only five minutes to <u>cover</u> the six blocks to the ball fields. "I have plenty of time. I guess I shouldn't have stayed to play that last game of checkers with grandpa," Ben thought out loud.

3. Coasting past a wooden fence, Ben turned onto a gravel path overgrown with weeds. He knew this shortcut would shave a couple of minutes off his travel time. However, he would have to ride over the old bridge that crossed the creek behind his house. The wooden planks that served as the floor were beginning to rot out. He knew he needed to be careful.

4. As Ben approached the bridge, he heard a low whimpering sound. At first he thought it was a squirrel up in the trees. But as he got closer to the bridge, Ben spotted a small dog stuck in a hole in one of the planks on the bridge. The dog was desperately <u>attempting</u> to grab hold of the plank from underneath. He kept trying this over and over again. The brown and white terrier was wedged in tight. He was unable to climb out or drop down.

5. Ben looked at his watch. If he kept going he would make the tryouts in time. If he stopped to help the dog, he would be late. He might even miss the tryouts completely. Ben heard another whimper and he knew what he would do. "I can try out later in the year," he muttered as he headed across the bridge toward the dog.

6. Carefully making his way, Ben checked each plank before putting his full weight down. "It's okay, fella" soothed Ben. "I'm here to help." The dog stopped whimpering. He kept his eyes glued to Ben. The dog even managed a little wag of his tail.

7. Ben finally reached the dog and began to pull pieces of rotted wood away from his body. Gradually, the wood's tight grip around the dog began to loosen. Ben grabbed him by the collar and pulled him up. The little dog took off across the bridge and landed safely on the other side.

8. Ben sat there on the bridge for a few minutes. He was suddenly very tired. Then Ben heard voices approaching from the other side of the bridge. He saw the dog, a man, and a young boy running

© 2013 Queue, Inc. All rights reserved.   Reproducing copyrighted material is against the law!

up the path to the bridge. The man scooped up the little dog and handed it to the boy at his side.

9. "Stay here, Lucky!" said the boy. The man looked up and saw Ben sitting next to the hole in the bridge. Realizing what had probably happened, the man waved at Ben.

10. "Did you find Lucky stuck in the bridge?" the man asked as he walked up to the bridge.

11. "Yes I did," Ben answered. "He was wedged in tight. All I did was pull him out."

12. "We really appreciate what you did for Lucky. It was very kind of you to stop to help him. Billy and I will never forget this," said the man.

13. "Yeah!" shouted Billy from the other side. "You saved Lucky. You are a hero!"

14. Smiling, the man continued, "This old bridge has been a danger for a long time. It needs to be fixed. The first thing I am going to do tomorrow is get the city maintenance department out here to see what it will take to repair this bridge. As mayor, I need to make sure this bridge is safe for all to use. Say, why aren't you trying out for the baseball teams? Everyone your age is over at the ball fields."

15. "I was on my way there when I saw your dog stuck in the bridge," Ben replied.

16. "I will speak to the coaches and make sure you get another chance to try out. You have a good excuse for not being there," said the mayor as he helped Ben off the bridge.

17. "Thanks, Mr. Mayor," Ben said. Lucky barked happily.

18. "And Lucky thanks you, too!" laughed the mayor.

My Notes About What I Am Reading

(Category 1 – 4 B – RS)

1 Which meaning best fits the way cover is used in paragraph 2?

  A To put something on
  B To travel over
  C To keep from harm
  D To take in

(Category 1 – 4 B – RS)

2 In paragraph 4, the word attempting means—

  A expecting.
  B moving.
  C trying.
  D waiting.

(Category 2 – Figure 19 D – RS)

3 Why is Ben careful as he walks across the bridge?

  A He does not want to scare the dog.
  B He does not want to fall through.
  C He does not want to hurt the dog.
  D He does not want to lose his way.

(Category 2 – 8 B – RS)

4 Which of these best tells how Billy feels about Ben?

  A Afraid
  B Disappointed
  C Impressed
  D Surprised

(Category 2 – 8 B – RS)

5 Which word best describes the mayor at the end of the story?

    A Bothered
    B Excited
    C Pleased
    D Worried

(Category 2 – 8 A - RS)

6 Before Ben walks out onto the bridge, what happens?

    A Ben hears a whimpering sound.
    B Lucky heads down the path toward home.
    C Ben pulls Lucky by the collar.
    D Lucky barks.

(Category 2 – 10 A - SS)

7 Read this sentence from the story.

    He kept his eyes glued to Ben.

The author uses these words to help the reader understand

    A how closely the dog watched Ben.
    B why the dog was afraid of Ben.
    C where Ben found the dog.
    D who happily thanked Ben for helping the dog.

Read the newspaper article before answering the questions below.

My Notes About What I Am Reading

BRUSHY CREEK WEEKLY

March 1 Issue
Volume 42

News from the Brushy Creek Neighborhood
Round Rock, Texas

Annual Neighborhood Book Sale
By Arthur Warren
Brushy Creek Staff Writer

1. The Brushy Creek Neighborhood Group will hold their Annual Neighborhood Book Sale on Saturday. It will be held at the neighborhood community center located at 500 Front Street. The sale will start at 9:00 a.m. and continue until 4:00 p.m. Monies raised by the book sale will be used to buy new books for the local branch of the public library.

2. Debra Calhoun is this year's chairperson of the book sale. When asked about the sale, Ms. Calhoun said, "This is our library's biggest fund raiser of the year. People gather their old or well-read books and donate them to the book sale. We have volunteers who come and sort the books, clean them, tape any tears or rips, and put them out for others to see. It takes a good three months to get ready. This year we hope to have over one thousand books for sale. Please come by on Saturday and support our library."

3. Dustin Martin has been a volunteer worker for the past five book sales. He helps sort the books as they arrive for the sale. He also helps people look for books the day of the sale. "I never get tired of helping at the book sale," Mr. Martin said. "I love to watch the faces of the little children when they pick up a book that is new to them. I see a sense of wonder and excitement. That makes all of the hard work getting everything ready for the sale worth it."

4. A reading fair will also take place during the book sale. Games, contests, and activities will be presented. They will teach parents and children about reading and writing. Students from Mrs. Albert's fifth grade class from Barker Elementary School will perform an original puppet show titled "The Fourth Billy Goat."

5. Mrs. Albert said, "The boys and girls worked really hard on their play. They wrote the play themselves. The class also made all of the puppets and scenery. Many hours of practice went into this play. We hope everyone from the community comes to the book sale and watches the play after buying books."

6   Parents from the Barker Elementary School Parent Group have spent the last two weekends walking the Brushy Creek Neighborhood. They have gone door-to-door handing out fliers and answering questions about the book sale.

7   One of the parents, Dorothy Smith, had this to say about the book sale: "This book sale really helps the people of Brushy Creek get to know each other. We come together to share our books and help our library. At the same time, we find out about our neighbors. Everyone has a good time."

8   The Brushy Creek Neighborhood Group will serve refreshments all throughout the book sale. If you would like to help with the refreshments or the book sale, or if you just have questions, please call Debra Calhoun at 555-1241.

My Notes About What I Am Reading

Kinds of Books Given for the Book Sale	Number of Books Given
Picture books	342
Poetry books	67
Mystery books	180
How-to books	46
Drawing books	24
Travel books	110
Science fiction books	375
Cooking books	80

(Category 3 – 15 B – SS)

1   According to the chart, the reader can tell that

   A   more drawing books were given to the sale than poetry books.
   B   more mysteries were given for the sale than any other kind of book.
   C   fewer picture books were given for the sale than how-to books.
   D   less than 100 poetry books were given for the sale.

(Category 3 – 13 B – RS)

2 Which sign was probably made by Debra Calhoun for the book sale on Saturday?

　　A Free Books! Come to Saturday's Book Sale!
　　B Book Sale Saturday! Help Your Local Library!
　　C Book Sale Saturday! Come and Help Clean Books!
　　D Free Writing Lessons! Come Learn at Saturday's Book Sale!

(Category 3 – 15 B – SS)

3 What can the reader tell about the books given for the book sale from the chart?

　　A Cooking books were the most given book for the sale.
　　B People gave the same number of mystery and travel books for the sale.
　　C People gave the same number of poetry and how-to books for the sale.
　　D Drawing books were the least given book for the sale.

(Category 3 – Figure 19 D – RS)

4 This article was written mainly to

　　A tell about a neighborhood book sale.
　　B tell about who comes to a book sale.
　　C explain how to run a book sale.
　　D explain why neighborhoods have a book sale.

(Category 3 – Figure 19 D – RS)

5   Which statement from the article shows the reader that a lot of work went into the book sale?

   A   "This is our library's biggest fund raiser of the year."
   B   The sale will start at 9:00 a.m. and continue until 4:00 p.m.
   C   It takes a good three months to get ready.
   D   "I never get tired of helping at the book sale."

(Category 3 – 13 A – RS)

6   Which detail listed below is important to the main idea of the passage?

   A   The community center is on Fourth Street.
   B   People have many well-read books.
   C   Book sale workers sort books for the sale.
   D   People of the neighborhood have questions about the book sale.

Read the passage "Janet's Diary" before answering the questions below.

My Notes About What I Am Reading

JANET'S DIARY

Janet spent one week at a camp during the summer. She decided to keep a diary of her time while at the camp.

Sunday

1. I can hardly believe it! We are finally here at camp. My mom and dad helped me unpack my things. I was a little nervous when they waved goodbye and drove away. But when I met the other girls in my cabin, I felt better. Nellie, Isabel, and Stacy all seem like nice caring people. I think we will get along just great! The first thing we had to do together was design and make a flag for our cabin. We had to find out all about each other and put some of those things in our flag. Isabel likes to ride horses. Stacy enjoys reading poetry. Nellie knows all about computers. We all like to work on jigsaw puzzles. The counselors here at camp wanted us to come up with a name for our cabin, too. We decided on "The Four Puzzlers."

Monday

2. Today we learned how to paddle and use canoes. First we found out how to wear a life jacket. This will help keep us floating if we end up in the water. Next we were taught how to <u>properly</u> hold the paddle. If it is held wrong, you might lose it in the water. Then our leader showed us how to sit in a canoe to keep our balance and not tip the canoe over. She taught us how to use most of our bodies to paddle the canoe through the water. Finally, we set the canoes into the lake and took off. We had a race to the island in the middle of the lake. My canoe came in second. I am very sore and tired. I am going to go to bed early tonight.

Tuesday

3. It rained all day. We stayed in and put puzzles together.

Wednesday

4. We spent the entire day working on helpful projects around the campgrounds. Each cabin was responsible to clean, repair, or tidy up an area of the camp. The Four Puzzlers had to clean up and

make ready the main campfire area where the food is cooked. Each of us gathered lots and lots of sticks and bigger pieces of wood. We set these down in big piles near the campfire. Nellie and Isabel made sure that the rocks used for seats were in rows and lined up. Stacy and I cleared a wide path all around the fire. The path had to be free of any leaves, twigs, or grass. It took us about two hours to finish the job. We talked about our families and schools the whole time. I think I am even more tired than I was two days ago!

Saturday

5   Today was the last day at camp for the summer! The whole camp came together around the big campfire. We sang the songs we had learned all week. The camp counselors put on skits about the week. The camp leader presented special awards. The Four Puzzlers received an award for the neatest cabin.

6   I cried when I said goodbye to Stacy, Isabel, and Nellie. We traded addresses and phone numbers. We promised we would write to each other every week. We also promised to come back to camp next year at the same time and be cabin mates again. I can't wait!

My Notes About What I Am Reading

(Category 2 – 8 A – RS)

1   Paragraph 4 is important to the passage because it tells

   A   what the girls did to help around the camp.
   B   why Janet gets along so well with her cabin mates.
   C   how the camp fire needs to look.
   D   who is in each girl's family back home.

(Category 2 – 8 B – RS)

2   Which word best describes how Janet felt about leaving camp on Saturday to go home?

   A   Afraid
   B   Excited
   C   Surprised
   D   Sad

(Category 1 – 4 B- RS)

3 In paragraph 2, the word <u>properly</u> means—

    A carefully.
    B correctly.
    C quietly.
    D suddenly.

(Category 2 – 2 B – SS)

4 What happens after the girls put the canoe in the water?

    A The canoes have a race to the island.
    B The girls learn how to keep the canoe from turning over.
    C The leader shows them how to hold a paddle.
    D The girls are told how to wear a life jacket.

(Category 2 – Figure 19 D – RS)

5 Why does the ground around the stones of the center of the camp's cooking spot have to be clear of grass and leaves?

    A To keep campers from tripping over them
    B To keep them from blowing in the food
    C To keep them to put in the fire
    D To keep them from catching on fire

(Category 2 – 8 A – RS)

6 Before Janet cries, what does she do?

    A Janet goes home.
    B Janet helps clean the camp.
    C Janet trades phone numbers with her friends.
    D Janet promises to write to people from the camp.

(Category 2 – 9 – SS)

7 The information in this passage helps the reader better understand Janet by

    A telling what Janet does while at camp.
    B describing what the camp looks like.
    C showing where the camp is found.
    D explaining how Janet makes friends at camp.

(Category 2 – 16 – SS)

8 The picture is included in this passage to

    A provide information to the reader about how best to ride in a canoe.
    B show the reader how a canoe is made.
    C show the reader how people fit in a canoe.
    D provide information to the reader about what a canoe and its paddles look like

Read the story "The Bus Ride" before answering the questions below.

THE BUS RIDE

1. "Here it comes!" Jack shouted. He leaped up from the bench and stared down the street. Quickly, Jack's mother took hold of his hand. It was not distrust. The rush of traffic was only a few feet away.

2. "Stay with me," Jack's mother said. "We have to make sure we get on this bus so we can visit grandma downtown at her shop for lunch. Be careful with your conduct. Please watch how you behave. I do not want you to get into trouble."

3. "Yes, ma'am," said Jack. He and his mother got in line between a man carrying a lot of packages and a woman holding a baby. The baby reached out to touch Jack's bright red hat. With hardly a sound, the baby grabbed Jack's hat and pulled it off.

4. "Hey!" laughed Jack. "I need that hat. Besides, it is too big for you."

5. "I am so sorry," said the woman holding the baby.

6. "That's okay, ma'am," replied Jack. "I think he just likes the color."

7. Shifting the baby to her other arm, the woman climbed up the bus steps. Once inside the bus the baby turned his attention to the bright blue hat of the bus driver. The mother had taken the seat right behind the driver.

8. "Come on, Jack," said his mother. They mounted the steps and dropped the bus fare into the coin slot. Then Jack's mother led him down the aisle to a pair of seats in front of the rear door of the long bus.

9. Jack took his seat next to the window. More people climbed aboard the bus. It looked like everyone wanted to go downtown at the same time.

10. The bus rumbled like the snoring of an old man. It moved along the street on its way toward the center of the city. Jack watched the cars and trucks as they passed by. He observed many stores and shops full of customers. He saw sidewalks with people crowded close together. Jack wondered where they were all going.

11. He asked his mother about the bus. "How many people can it hold? Does it go back and forth on the same street all day? How old do you have to be to be a bus driver? What happens if it breaks down?" She tried to answer him as best as she could. Each of her answers seemed to lead to more questions from Jack.

My Notes About What I Am Reading

12 Finally, Jack's mother shook his shoulder and whispered, "We get off at the next stop. Let's stand up and get ready to leave."

13 Jack and his mother made their way toward the back door of the bus. She reached up and pulled on a thin cord that ran along the top of the windows. A soft "ding" could be heard. The bus immediately slowed down. The driver swerved to the right and pulled up to the corner. A hiss of the brakes signaled the bus' stopping. The back door swung open and Jack stepped onto the sidewalk. His mother followed close behind.

14 Jack looked up just in time to see the door of the bus close. In another moment, the bus had pulled away from the corner and was weaving its way farther into the city.

15 "Hi, Mona! Hi, Jack!" said a voice over the roar of the city. Jack turned and saw his grandmother walking towards them. "How was the bus ride?" she asked as she cradled his face in her hands. Bending down she gave Jack a quick kiss on his forehead. Then she hugged his mother.

16 "It felt like a car built to hold four people trying to carry eight people, Mama," replied Jack's mother.

17 "Well, now you two are here with me. We will have a nice lunch and enjoy our time together before I have to get back to work. I came into work early today so I can have an extra-long lunch," said Jack's grandmother.

18 Jack and his mother smiled. He liked spending time with his grandmother. As the three made their way toward the restaurant, Jack noticed another bus heading away from the city. Already he couldn't wait for the ride home.

My Notes About What I Am Reading

(Category 1 – 4 C – SS)

1 In paragraph 10, which word means about the same as <u>observed</u>?

    A Passed
    B Rumbled
    C Watched
    D Wondered

(Category 2 – 8 B – RS)

2 How does Jack feel about his grandmother at the end of the story?

    A Jack hopes his grandmother will be safe.
    B Jack likes his grandmother's cooking.
    C Jack enjoys his grandmother's company.
    D Jack thinks his grandmother spends too much time with him.

(Category 2 – 8 B – RS)

3 How does Jack feel as he is riding on the bus?

    A Curious about the bus
    B Disappointed about his seat
    C Worried about his mother
    D Surprised about where the bus is going

(Category 2 – Figure 19 D – RS)

4 Why does Jack's mother hold his hand as they get on the bus?

    A So he will get in line.
    B So he will not go out into the street.
    C So it will be easier to get on the bus.
    D So it will not leave without them.

(Category 2 – 10 A – SS)

5 Which words from the passage help the reader hear the bus that Jack rides downtown?

    A With hardly a sound
    B The snoring of an old man
    C Shook his shoulder and whispered
    D Over the roar of the city

(Category 2 – 10 A – SS)

6 Read this sentence from the passage.

> *"It felt like a car built to hold four people trying to carry eight people, Mama," replied Jack's mother.*

The author uses these words to help the reader make a picture of

    A the time the bus took to move slowly along the street.
    B how often the bus stopped so people could get on or off.
    C how crowded the bus was.
    D why the bus went to the downtown part of the city.

(Category 2 – 16 – SS)

7 The picture is included in the passage to

    A explain why Jack and his mother are riding the bus.
    B show who rides the bus to the middle of the city.
    C provide information about how fast buses move from place to place.
    D show where Jack and his mother catch the bus.

Read the story "What's for Dessert?" before answering the questions below.

My Notes About What I Am Reading

WHAT'S FOR DESSERT?

1. Bradley sat in front of his bedroom window and looked out. He was deep in thought. His best friend, Jason, sat on the bed, tossing a basketball into the air.

2. "What are you going to do?" asked Jason.

3. "I'm not sure," answered Bradley. "I'm still thinking. Do you have any ideas?"

4. "Sure. I want you to have chocolate ice cream and chocolate cake with chocolate icing," replied Jason.

5. Bradley turned around and looked straight at Jason. "You know we can't have those things. This is supposed to be a health fair, not a chocolate fair. I need to come up with a healthy dessert that everyone will eat. I thought this job would be easy. Now I'm not so sure. I need some more suggestions."

6. "What about vanilla ice cream and vanilla cake with vanilla icing?" said Jason with a big grin across his face.

7. "Come on, Jason," scowled Bradley. "Let's get serious."

8. "Okay," said Jason.

9. The two boys sat and quietly thought. Suddenly, Jason stopped tossing the basketball into the air.

10. "I've got it!" he shouted. "Brussels sprouts! They're healthy!"

11. Bradley grabbed his head with both hands and moaned like a baby missing a favorite toy, "This is <u>impossible</u>. Why did I volunteer for this job? Today is Friday and the fair is tomorrow. It's only one day away and I have no idea what to have for dessert. I've still got all of the signs to make. This job is a lot harder than I thought it would be."

12. "I'm sorry, Bradley," said Jason. "I've got to go. My mom wants me home by 5:00 for my piano lesson. I'll see you tomorrow."

13. Bradley waved goodbye to Jason and turned toward the window. Across the street, dozens of orange trees moved back and forth in the south Texas breeze. Once again Bradley became lost in his thoughts.

14. Saturday dawned bright and sunny. Sunlight streamed into Bradley's upstairs bedroom window like a flashlight into a dark

room. He had not slept well. He had tossed and turned all night worrying about what to do for dessert for the health fair. Bradley sat up in bed, slumped over, and rubbed his eyes. He glanced out of the window, his attention caught by a quick flash of orange. Like a hound after a rabbit, Bradley moved closer to his window.

15 "That's it!" he cried. "That will make a great dessert! Mom! Mom!" Bradley yelled down to his mother.

16 "What is it, dear?" answered Mrs. Mallard.

17 "I know what to have for dessert at the health fair," panted Bradley coming down the stairs out of breath.

18 "Good, dear. I was getting worried I might have to step in and come up with an idea myself," said Bradley's mother. She was working on information packets for the health fair at the kitchen table. "What did you decide?"

19 "Wait and you will see. Right now I've got signs to make," replied Bradley, heading out the door.

20 "Bradley, shouldn't you get out of your pajamas and put on some regular clothes?" mentioned his mother as he passed by.

21 "Oh, right, Mom," said Bradley looking down at his pajamas. He headed back upstairs. Two minutes later, he rushed back by his mother and out the back door. He had put on a red shirt, blue pants, and socks with shoes that did not match. "See you in a bit, Mom. I'll be down at the old shed making signs," Bradley hollered over his shoulder.

22 Turning back to her work Mom wondered out loud, "What did he come up with for dessert?"

23 The turnout for the health fair was more than expected. Held across the street from Bradley's house, the trees that covered the large field provided much needed space. Mrs. Mallard had seen Bradley at the start of the fair. He still had not told her what he had thought of for dessert.

24 "Look for the signs," is all he said to her.

25 Mrs. Mallard had not been able to get away to look. She was not trying to hide. She had been too busy handing out information packets to the health fair visitors. However, now that her job was winding down, she wanted to know where Bradley was. She went to seek him out. Turning the corner by the food tent, she finally saw one of Bradley's signs. As she read she exclaimed, "Of course! That's so simple! What a great idea for a dessert! Good job, Bradley!"

My Notes About What I Am Reading

(Category 1 – 4 A – RS)

1   If "possible" means "able to be", then impossible, as used in paragraph 11, would mean

   A   Sometimes able to be
   B   Able to be again
   C   Not able to be
   D   Able to be before

(Category 1 – 4 C – SS)

2   Which word below means the opposite of the word <u>busy</u> in paragraph 25?

   A   Happy
   B   Idle
   C   Lost
   D   Lonely

(Category 2 - 8 A – RS)

3   Why is paragraph 5 important to the story?

   A   It tells why Jason has to go home.
   B   It tells why Jason's mother has to work at the health fair.
   C   It explains that Jason needs to find a way to make signs for the dessert.
   D   It explains that Jason needs to think of a dessert for the fair.

(Category 2 – Figure 19 E – RS)

4 Read the first sentence of the summary below to answer the next question.

> **Summary**
> Jason tries to help Bradley think of what to have for dessert at the health fair.

Which sentences complete the summary?

A Bradley plays with Jason. Jason has to go home because he has a piano lesson.
B Bradley worries about what to have for dessert. He comes up with an idea. Bradley gets ready for the health fair.
C Bradley goes to bed without a plan. He wakes up with a new plan and jumps out of bed. He goes downstairs to get started.
D Bradley does not sleep well. He sees his mom the day of the health fair. She is going to give out information packets to visitors.

(Category 2 – Figure 19 D – RS)

5 Which sentence from the story shows that Bradley has decided what to have as a dessert at the health fair?

A "I'll be down at the old shed making signs."
B "This job is a lot harder than I thought it would be."
C Bradley grabbed his head with both hands and moaned.
D Once again Bradley became lost in his thoughts.

(Category 2 – Figure 19 D – RS)

6 Why did Bradley jump out of bed on Saturday morning?

    A He was late for the health fair.
    B He thought of what to have for dessert.
    C He needed to help his mom at the health fair.
    D He was tired of staying in bed thinking about dessert.

(Category 2 – 10 A – SS)

7 Which words in the passage help the reader know how Bradley sounded after Jason said that Bradley needs to have brussel sprouts for the health fair?

    A Turned toward the window
    B Moved back and forth
    C Like a baby missing a favorite toy
    D Like a flashlight into a dark room

(Category 2 – 10 A – SS)

8 Read this sentence from the story.

> **Like a hound after a rabbit, Bradley moved closer to his window.**

The author uses these words to help the reader understand

    A the way Bradley moved to the window.
    B when Bradley moved to the window.
    C what Bradley saw through the window.
    D the reason Bradley moved to the window.

Read the article "The Power of the Wind" before answering the questions below.

My Notes About What I Am Reading

THE POWER OF THE WIND

1. Have you ever tried to fly a kite on a windy day? Or tried to rake leaves into a pile when the wind is blowing strongly? Maybe you have had your umbrella almost torn out of your grip while walking on a stormy day? If you have ever experienced any of these things, you know of the powerful force that the wind can have.

The Wind Moved Ships

2. People have tried to use the force that blowing wind brings for many hundreds of years. Ancient sailors knew the power that comes from the wind. They successfully used its strength to move ships across lakes and oceans. Ships used simple cloth sails to push them in the direction the wind blew. Later, sailors were able to discover how to sail into the wind. Sailing ships were used less often when engines powered by fossil fuels were invented. Sailing ships are still around today. Lightweight plastic sails help push some of these ships through the water.

Early Windmills Used the Wind

3. One of the earliest machines to use the power of the wind on land was the windmill. It was used to grind grain into flour. Some windmills were also used to pump water. They helped bring water from rivers to thirsty lands. Windmills first appeared in the Middle East and later spread to the Far East and Europe.

4. The first windmills used sails like those found on sailing ships. Later, windmills in Europe used wooden arms attached to a center post. The sails attached to the arms would catch the wind, which caused them to move. A set of wheels allowed the spinning action of the sails to turn heavy round stones. Grain was put in between the stones and crushed into flour. This flour was then used to make bread.

The Sails on Windmills

5. The sails of early windmills could be changed for the speed of the wind. If the wind was strong, the sails could open to let some of the wind through. This slowed the sails down. The sails could also be closed so that the slower wind pushed against the whole sail. This made the sails go around faster.

6   The part of the windmill that held the sails could even be moved so that it was always facing into the wind. This allowed the windmills to be used no matter what the wind direction.

A Change

7   Before windmills, water was used to turn grain into flour. Water mills could only be put next to running water. Most often, the rivers or streams that supplied the running water were controlled by powerful land owners. They could choose who built a water mill. Windmills could be built anywhere. They could be used by less powerful people. The common people were able to decide more things about their lives. They began to have more control.

Windmills of North America

8   Windmills in North America had a different look than those found in other parts of the world. Instead of four large blades, the windmills that dotted Canada and the United States used many small wooden or metal blades. These wind machines were used by farmers to pump water out of the ground. The water was used on farmland. Windmills were also used to bring water to cattle that fed on the open countryside.

Windmills of Today

9   Many of today's windmills are used to make electricity. Called "wind turbines", they are much larger and more powerful than earlier windmills. Most have two or three long thin blades that sit on top of tall towers. Some are over three hundred feet tall. They often use computers to decide how to turn. The blades are connected to a generator. The generator makes the electricity. The electricity travels along wires from the wind turbine to wherever needed.

10   Most of the electricity that is made around the world is still made by burning fossil fuels such as oil, gas, and coal. Energy made by wind machines costs more than energy made by fossil fuels. As improvements are made, the amount of money needed to use the wind to make energy will not be as much as it is now. More countries will use windmills.

11   Sometimes many wind turbines are put together. These are called "wind farms". Used together, these wind turbines can make enough electricity for a whole town.

12   Energy made by the wind does not make pollution. The wind is free and it will not run out like fossil fuels will. The hope is that we will be able to make more energy and less pollution from the never-ending power of the wind.

My Notes About What I Am Reading

Early Uses of the Wind by People

To crush grain to make flour
To pump water for crops
To pump water for cattle
To move ships
To fly kites

Later Uses of the Wind by People

To make electricity

Where Windmills Have Been Found	What Windmills Do There
Middle East	Grind grain, pump water for land
Far East	Grind grain, pump water for land
Europe	Grind grain, pump water for land, make electricity
North America	Grind grain, pump water for land and animals, make electricity

My Notes About What I Am Reading

(Category 3 – Figure 19 D – RS)

1 The article was written mainly to

    A tell what a windmill does to make flour.
    B explain how a windmill makes electricity.
    C tell how people have used wind to do work.
    D explain why wind power will help save energy.

(Category 1 – 4 C – SS)

2 In paragraph 3, which word means about the same as <u>pump</u>?

    A Use
    B Bring
    C Appeared
    D Grind

(Category 3 – 13 D – RS)

3 Which of the following from the passage would help the reader find information about windmills in the United States?

    A The Wind Moves Things
    B Early Windmills Use the Wind
    C The Sails on Windmills
    D Windmills of North America

(Category 3 – 15 B – SS)

4. According to the charts, what was a later use of wind by people?

   A   To pump water for crops
   B   To crush grain for flour
   C   To make electricity
   D   To move ships

Category 3 – 13 B – RS)

5   Which sentence from the passage lets the reader know that electricity made with the wind will cost less in the future?

   A   As improvements are made, the amount of money needed to use the wind to make energy will not be as much as it is now.
   B   Most of the electricity that is made around the world is still made by burning fossil fuels such as oil, gas, and coal.
   C   Many of today's windmills are used to make electricity.
   D   Energy made by the wind does not make pollution.

(Category 3 – 15 B – SS)

6 According to the passage and the charts, where are windmills used to make electricity?

    A Far East
    B Middle East
    C Europe
    D Antarctica

(Category 3 – 16 – SS)

7 The picture next to paragraphs 3 and 4 is included to show the

    A places windmills were used in Europe.
    B speed of the arms on a windmill.
    C pump that was used to grind grain into flour.
    D number of arms on windmills found in Europe.

(Category 3 – Figure 19 D – RS)

8 From information found in the passage, the reader can tell that windmills

    A helped people be more in charge of their lives.
    B were easy for people to build and run.
    C were hard to fix once broken.
    D cost a lot of money and took a long time to build.

(Category 3 – Figure 19 E – RS)

9 Which is the best summary of the passage?

    A People have sailed ships for many years. Wind pushed against sails made of cloth to move the ships through the water. Later ships used engines to move through the water. Some ships use plastic sails.

    B People have used the wind to move ships and turn windmills. Windmills have been used to grind grain and pump water. Blades made of cloth, wood, or metal are turned by the wind. Windmills known as "wind turbines" are also able to make electricity.

    C Windmills that make electricity are sometimes called "wind turbines". These big machines turn in the wind and make electricity used by homes and businesses. This electricity costs a lot of money. The costs are becoming less expensive.

    D Windmills have arms that turn in the wind. Some windmills have three, four, or more arms. Some of the arms are made of wood. Other arms are made of metal or cloth. Windmills have been used for many years.

Read the article "They Fall From the Sky" before answering the questions below.

My Notes About What I Am Reading

THEY FALL FROM THE SKY

1. A fire spreads quickly through the thick forest. Gusty winds push the flames along the ground covered with dry grass, leaves, and twigs. Thick smoke fills the air and blocks out the sky. The entire forest is in danger of burning. Strong winds threaten to blow the flames into other surrounding forests.

2. A wildfire has started burning everything in its path. It is out of control. The fire is soon spotted by a fire spotter watching from a high tower. The fire is burning in a part of the forest where there are no roads. Regular firefighters are not able to get to the fire. A special group of people known as "smokejumpers" are needed to fight this fire.

3. Smokejumpers are firefighters who parachute from an airplane. They fly over the fire looking for the best place to land. The smokejumpers jump and land on the ground. The airplane drops supplies and equipment to fight the fire. The smokejumpers gather what is needed and head for the fire. Their backpacks may weigh over 100 pounds. The smokejumpers may need to walk many miles across dangerous ground to get to the fire.

4. Once at the fire, the smokejumpers get busy trying to stop the fire from moving. One of the first things they do is make a safety zone. This is a place that the smokejumpers can go to get away from the fire in an emergency. The leader makes sure each smokejumper knows where the safety zone is and how to get to it.

5. If smokejumpers do get trapped by a fire, they are able to use a fire shelter. This is a special tent made of fire-resistant material. It does not burn easily. A firefighter can crawl into this tent and be kept safe from the flames. The firefighter lies down looking at the ground. The tent holds a small amount of cooler air. This lets the firefighter breathe. The firefighter stays inside the tent until the fire has passed and it is cool enough to leave.

6. Smokejumpers start fighting a fire by making a "fireline". This is a wide space of land that has been cleared of everything down to the ground. The firefighters hope to keep the fire from spreading past this fireline. Many hours of hard work go into making a fire-

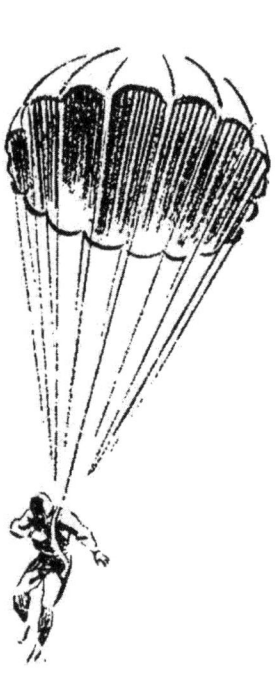

line. Trees have to be cut down. The ground has to be dug up to get rid of all things that burn.

7   Sometimes the smokejumpers start fires to help stop a fire. These are called "backfires". They burn between the fireline and the big fire that is coming. Smokejumpers want to burn away any parts of the forest that the bigger fire could use as fuel. The firefighters hope this will slow or stop the fire from going any farther.

8   When the fire has been stopped moving, the firefighters have to put it out. Airplanes and helicopters help with this part of the job. They carry large amounts of water that can be dropped onto the fire to put out the flames.

9   The fire is out! Now the smokejumpers can get a few hours of much-needed rest. They grab a bite to eat from food they brought with them. They sleep for a couple of hours in sleeping bags. Then they wake up and make sure that the fire is completely out. The firefighters check for any spots that may still be burning. When the firefighters are satisfied that the fire is totally out, they can leave. They will probably walk many miles before they can be picked up and taken back to their base.

10 The smokejumpers do not get much rest back at their base. No matter what happened at the previous fire, they need to be ready for the next fire. The smokejumpers never know when the next call to fight a fire will come. The firefighters check and pack their parachutes. Equipment is cleaned. New supplies are set out for the next fire. The firefighters exercise each day to stay in shape. They are always training and learning how to be better smoke-jumpers. During the long fire season the smokejumpers may have to go back to fight many fires.

11 Smokejumpers think that they have the best job in firefighting. Ever on the ready, smokejumpers understand that they help keep the forests safe.

My Notes About What I Am Reading

(Category 3 – 13 C – RS)

1   Smokejumpers start fires

   A   to help stop a fire.
   B   to show where they need to be picked up.
   C   because they have run out of water.
   D   because there are no roads.

(Category 3 – Figure 19 D – RS)

2 The author wrote this article to

    A tell why people become smokejumpers.
    B explain the job of smokejumpers.
    C show the cause of forest fires.
    D describe what helicopters do to fight forest fires.

(Category 1 – 4 B – RS)

3 What does the word previous mean in paragraph 10?

    A Starting quickly
    B Causing
    C Happening before
    D Waiting

(Category 3 – 13 B – RS)

4 The reader can tell that

    A fewer and fewer fire fighters are becoming smokejumpers.
    B smokejumpers spend a lot of time in school training to be special firefighters.
    C it takes many years for fire fighters to become smokejumpers.
    D smokejumpers have to be ready to go to a fire in a moment's notice.

(Category 3 – Figure 19 E – RS)

5 A student is writing a summary of the article. Read the first two sentences below.

> **Summary**
> A fire starts in a forest.
> Smokejumpers go to the fire.

Which group of sentences best finishes the summary?

A They build a safety zone. The smokejumpers make sure that the flames are completely out.
B They walk many miles to do their job. Smokejumpers use a fire shelter to keep safe.
C They work together to put out the flames. Smokejumpers get ready for the next fire.
D They unpack their supplies and try to fight the fire. They stop the fire from spreading.

(Category 3 – Figure 19 D – RS)

6 Which sentence from the article shows that smokejumpers know their job is important?

A Once at the fire, the smokejumpers get busy trying to stop the fire from moving.
B Smokejumpers are firefighters who parachute from an airplane.
C Smokejumpers start fighting a fire by making a "fireline".
D Ever on the ready, smokejumpers understand that they help keep the forests safe.

Read the article "He Found What Was Special" before answering the questions below.

My Notes About What I Am Reading

HE FOUND WHAT WAS SPECIAL

A Hard Beginning

1. As a boy, Langston Hughes read about many faraway places. He longed to visit them. Born in Joplin, Missouri on February 1, 1902, his early life was hard. His father left his mother and moved to Mexico. Langston's mother worked many different jobs to have enough money to live. Langston's father, James Hughes, sent for his family to come live with him in Mexico. As soon as Langston and his mother arrived, an earthquake shook the town. This frightened Mrs. Hughes. She took Langston and returned to the United States right away.

2. Mrs. Hughes had to work at many jobs. She had a difficult time making enough money to even buy food. Langston went to live with his grandmother in Kansas. He was eight years old.

Living in Kansas

3. Langston loved his grandmother. She told him many wonderful stories about famous African Americans. The story that Langston enjoyed the most was about his grandfather, Lewis Sheridan Leary. Mr. Leary and others had helped people who were slaves fight to be free. Langston was very proud of his grandfather.

4. Langston felt lonely when he lived with his grandmother even though she cared for him well. He began to read about many people and places. Some were far away. Langston also began to write stories and poems.

Growing Up in Cleveland

5. When he was twelve years old, his grandmother died. He went back with his mother. They moved to Illinois. Then his family moved to Cleveland, Ohio. He was fourteen years old. There Langston went to high school. He enjoyed being in Cleveland. There were many other children from different countries and races.

6. While at the high school in Cleveland, Langston wrote more poems and stories. Some were published in the school magazine. He decided that he really enjoyed writing. He wrote about what he saw and felt around him. Langston wanted to write more one day.

7. The summer before his last year of high school, Langston's father sent for him. Mr. Hughes was still living in Mexico. Langston spent

the whole summer with his father. Langston learned that his father was not a happy person. He said and did things that were not nice to other people. Langston was glad to return to Cleveland.

A Chance to Go to College

8 Langston's father wanted him to come back to Mexico after Langston was finished with high school. Langston wanted to go to college, but he did not have enough money. He went to Mexico hoping his father would help send him to college. Mr. Hughes agreed to do this. He wanted Langston to become a mining engineer. They finally decided to have Langston <u>attend</u> Columbia University in New York City. Langston would go there in the fall.

9 A community of African Americans lived near the university. Langston enjoyed visiting with the people of this place called Harlem. He wrote about their lives. He wanted others to know of their happy times and sad times.

Wanting to Be a Writer

10 Soon he quit the university. He tried to find a job. He wanted to be a writer. Langston had a hard time finding a writing job. He finally got a job on a ship that was going to Africa. Langston met many different people in Africa.

11 When Langston returned to the United States, he lived in Washington, D. C. He worked at a hotel cleaning dishes from tables. One day a famous poet, Vachel Lindsay, sat at one of Langston's tables. Langston quickly wrote down some of his poems. He put them near Mr. Lindsay's plate. Mr. Lindsay read them. Mr. Lindsay said that Langston was a good poet. Soon there was a newspaper story about a new poet, Langston Hughes.

Life as a Writer

12 Langston Hughes continued to write poems and stories. His first book, *The Weary Blues*, was published in 1926. The poems in this book were about the interesting people of Harlem.

13 During the next years of his life, Langston wrote many more poems, stories, and books. He also wrote plays. He wrote about the happy and sad times of people. He wrote about the good and the bad times that people had during their lives. He made them special.

14 Langston Hughes died in 1967. But he had told his friends not to be sad. He wanted them to be happy and remember that each of their own lives was special.

(Category 1 – 4 B – RS)

1 In paragraph 8, which words help the reader know what the word <u>attend</u> means?

    A Would go there
    B Finally decided
    C Enough money
    D Finished with high school

(Category 2 – 8 A – RS)

2 Mrs. Hughes left Mexico when Langston was a boy because

    A there were no jobs.
    B Langston's father had moved away.
    C an earthquake shook the land.
    D Langston's grandmother had died.

(Category 2 – 2 B – SS)

3 Which of the following sections of the article would help the reader find information about Langston's grandmother?

    A A Hard Beginning
    B Living in Kansas
    C Growing Up in Cleveland
    D A Chance to Go to College

(Category 2 – 8 A – RS)

4 Langston moved back to Mexico after high school to

    A get money to go to college.
    B find a job.
    C live with his mother.
    D write a book.

(Category 2 – Figure 19 D – SS)

5 The article was written mainly to

    A explain what a poet does.
    B tell what a poet likes to write about.
    C show how to become a poet.
    D tell about the life of a poet.

(Category 2 – 9 – SS)

6 The information found in this passage helps the reader better understand Langston Hughes by

    A telling about his interest in being a mining engineer.
    B explaining who he went to school with as a young boy.
    C describing his early life.
    D showing some of his poems.

Read the article "Silk Spinners" before answering the questions below.

My Notes About What I Am Reading

SILK SPINNERS

1 A single silent shadow arches across the quiet morning air. Light catches the <u>slim</u> strand and it sparkles like a river of diamonds. Suddenly, the narrow line pulls taut as it snags a fluttering butterfly. The startled butterfly struggles to break free. The strong sticky thread is <u>unyielding</u>. The butterfly quickly becomes food for one of nature's silk spinners, the spider. Many of the insects spiders dine on are harmful to plants people enjoy.

2 Spiders are one of Earth's eight-legged wonders. They use their sticky tool of silk for many different jobs. Although most spiders are harmless to people, many people will scream, run the other way, and stay as far from spiders as possible. All spiders use silk in some way. Produced inside their bodies as a liquid, the silk comes out from under the backside. Once it hits the outside air, it dries into a narrow silk strand.

3 One of the most amazing jobs for a spider's silk is as a web. Spiders will build fancy webs using their silk. Lines of the sticky thread will be stretched across rocks, between branches of bushes, and in corners of rooms. Many of these places are high above the ground. Small insects creep, crawl, or fly into these hard-to-see webs. Once trapped, they have little chance of escaping. The web's maker may eat its catch right away. Sometimes it saves it until a later time.

4 Spider webs can be made in many different shapes. Garden spiders make round webs. Some spiders make webs in the form of a triangle. Others are made to look like a rectangle. A few spiders even build webs in the shape of funnels or tubes.

5 Do spiders get stuck in their own web? No. They have an oily covering on their bodies that keeps them from getting stuck. Some of the threads that they weave are dry. They do not have to worry about sticking as long as they are able to remember which threads are sticky and which are not.

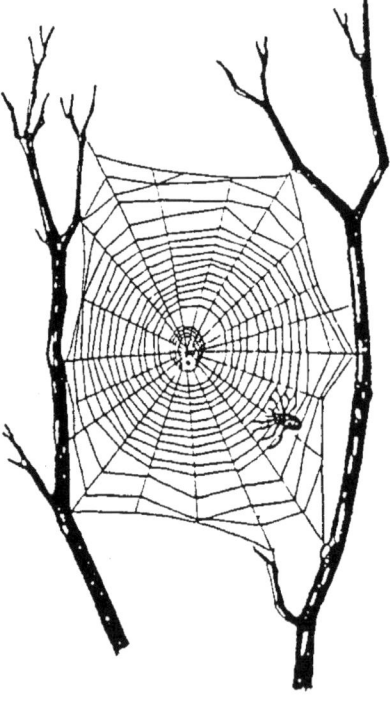

6 Watch for spider webs on your next trip outside. Then sit back and wait. You may be treated to an amazing view of one of nature's busy builders.

7 Spiders have enemies. These animals will often try to trap the spiders. The spiders give themselves a quick <u>escape</u>. They trail a line of their silk behind themselves as they skitter along the ground or sail through the air. They can easily retrace their path back home. This lifeline comes in handy.

8 Mother spiders use silk to wrap their eggs for protection. Inside the soft silk, the eggs begin to hatch into baby spiderlings. Some spiders attach the silk egg to a plant. They guard it until the babies are born. Others carry the eggs with them. Once the young spiderlings hatch, they are on their own. The young spiders begin spinning their own silk threads.

My Notes About What I Am Reading

(Category 1 – 4 B – RS)

1 In paragraph 1, the word <u>slim</u> means

    A bright.
    B clear.
    C thin.
    D tight.

(Category 1 – 4 A – RS)

2 The word "yielding" means giving. What does <u>unyielding</u> mean in paragraph 1?

    A Giving again
    B Sometimes giving
    C Not giving
    D Giving before

(Category 3 – 13 A – RS)

3   Which detail sentence from the passage is important to the main idea of the passage?

   A   Then sit back and wait.
   B   They use their sticky tool of silk for many different jobs.
   C   Others carry the eggs with them.
   D   Many of these places are high above the ground.

(Category 3 –Figure 19 D – RS)

4   Read this sentence from the passage.

> **Although most spiders are harmless to people, many people will scream, run the other way, and stay as far from spiders as possible.**

The reader can tell from this information that

   A   Some people are afraid of spiders.
   B   Some people have spiders as pets.
   C   Spiders live in people's gardens.
   D   Spiders are able to move quickly.

(Category 1 – 4 C – RS)

5   In paragraph 7, which word means the opposite of <u>escape</u>?

   A   Give
   B   Sail
   C   Trail
   D   Trap

(Category 3 – 13 B – RS)

6   Reread paragraph 7. The reader can tell from this information that spiders use their silk to

    A get away from other animals.
    B build homes.
    C find other spiders.
    D keep plants alive and safe.

(Category 3 – Figure 19 E – RS)

7   Which is the best summary of the passage?

    A Spiders make silk from inside of their bodies. This silk sticks to rocks, trees, and other plants. The silk is made into a web that traps insects. Spiders eat the insects right away or save them to eat at a later time.
    B Spiders use silk to make sticky webs. The webs are used to catch other small animals. These small animals are the spiders' food.
    C Spiders are eight-legged animals that make silk. Spiders use the silk to make webs that trap food. Silk is used to help them get away from enemies. Spiders use silk to take care of their young. The young grow up and make their own silk.
    D Spiders use silk to keep their eggs safe. Some spiders carry their eggs with them while others stick the eggs on a plant to stay safe. The baby spiders come out of their eggs and go off to live on their own.

(Category 3 – 16 – SS)

8   The author includes the picture in the passage to

    A show what a spider catches in its web.
    B provide information about how a spider makes a web.
    C explain why spiders build a web.
    D show how a spider attaches its web to plants.

Read the story "Maria's Idea" before answering the questions below.

MARIA'S IDEA

1. "Mom! My bike's busted again!" whined Maria as she slammed open the back door. "My tire is as flat as a pancake. This is the third time this month and it's only the third week.

2. "Well, honey, you just have to keep patching it until you are able to buy a new tube to go inside the tire. Your dad and I bought the last four tubes. We decided that you needed to pay for the next one," replied Mom.

3. "Yeah, I know, Mom," sighed Maria. "But I don't have any more allowance and there is only one more patch. That tube has more patches on it than a worn-out pair of jeans."

4. "I'm sorry, Maria," answered Mom. "It would probably help if you would quit riding through the back field. You know it has lots of stickers and plants with thorns."

5. "That field is the quickest way home from school. If I go the other way, it takes me ten more minutes to get home," said Maria as she plopped down into a chair at the table. "I have to get to soccer practice early every day to help my coach set up. She said that without my help she wouldn't be able to get everything ready on time."

6. Mom turned to Maria and, looking squarely into her eyes, said, "It sure looks like we have a problem to solve."

7. Maria blinked and replied, "Okay, Mom. I'll stop complaining and figure a way to solve this problem. First, I have to get to practice and then finish my homework."

8. Later that evening, Maria came downstairs, through the hall, and into the living room. "Mom and Dad, I think I may have an answer to my bike problem."

9. "Wow! That was quick," said Mom scooting to the edge of her seat. "What do you have in mind?"

10. "I am going to stop taking the shortcut home through the back field. I will come home the front way. I will stop talking with my friends for so long after school. This will get me home about the same time as before so I can get over to help my coach set up for practice. Then, I'm going to get a part-time job on the weekends. I'll earn money to get a new tube for my bike tire. Maybe I will make enough to buy new goal-keeper gloves and help our team," Maria said.

My Notes About What I Am Reading

11 "Do you think you can handle the responsibility of working for someone?" asked Dad.

12 "Well, I help my coach get ready for practice. I do my chores here everyday. Yes, I think I can handle it," replied Maria.

13 "How are you going to find a job?" asked Mom.

14 "I will make signs and put them up all over the neighborhood. They will let people know I can do odd jobs on the weekends. Spring Break is coming up next week. I think people will be cleaning their houses and yards. I can help them haul their old stuff to the dump, weed their gardens, or anything else they need," said Maria.

15 Mom and Dad sat silent for a moment. Maria could not sit still in her chair. Then Dad glanced at Mom and Maria thought she saw her dad wink.

16 "Okay, Maria. Put up your signs. Let's see what happens," said Dad.

17 Maria jumped up, looking like a jack-in-the-box. "Great! I'll get right on those signs. Tomorrow is Tuesday. Maybe there will be a job by the weekend."

18 Maria put up her signs the next day after practice. Wednesday and Thursday came and went. No job. No one even called.

19 There was no practice on Friday. Maria came home after school and rushed in to ask her mom if anyone had called about a job.

20 "As a matter of fact, there was one call just before you came home," explained Mom. "Here's the phone number."

21 Maria grabbed the paper from her mom's hand and rushed to the phone. She quickly pushed in the numbers and waited.

22 "Hello, my name is Maria Santos. You called earlier about wanting me to work for you?" Maria almost shouted into the phone. Then she stopped. "Dad, is that you? Did I dial your number by mistake? Wait a minute. This is the number Mom wrote down. What? This is no mistake? Uh…Okay…Sure…Yes. Bye, Dad."

23 Maria hung up the phone. Turning to her mom, she said, "Mom, did you know about this?"

My Notes About What I Am Reading

© 2013 Queue, Inc. All rights reserved.   43   Reproducing copyrighted material is against the law!

24 "Yes, dear. We have wanted to have you work at our shop for a while. But we were not sure you would be ready and willing. Now we think you are," said Mom as she gave Maria a big hug.

25 "Thanks, Mom," said Maria. "Let's make a list of what I can help with at the shop."

My Notes About What I Am Reading

(Category 2 – Figure 19 D – RS)

1 Read the signs below to answer the following question.

1

Hard-working girl looking for weekend work!

Call: 555-1246

2

Willing to work for free!

Call: 555-1246

3

Know of anyone looking for a part-time job?

Call: 555-1246

4

Need some helpful tips on how to clean your house or yard?

Call: 555-1246

Which sign was probably made by Maria to help her get a job?

- A Sign 1
- B Sign 2
- C Sign 3
- D Sign 4

(Category 2 – 2 B – RS)

2. What is Maria's problem in the story?

    A   She wants to find a new glove.
    B   She wants to get a job to fix her bike.
    C   She is late for soccer practice.
    D   She is having a hard time with her homework.

(Category 2 – 10 A – SS)

3. Which words from the story help the reader see what Maria's bicycle tire looks like at the beginning of the story?

    A   New tube
    B   Edge of her seat
    C   As flat as a pancake
    D   Like a jack-in-the-box

(Category 2 – 5 A – SS)

4. The theme of the story is

    A   be willing and ready and work will come.
    B   let friends help you get a job.
    C   keep your family happy.
    D   practice makes prefect.

(Category 1 – 4 C – SS)

5 Which word from the story means to carry?

    A For
    B Four
    C Hall
    D Haul

(Category 2 – Figure 19 E – RS)

6 Which of these gives the best summary for the story?

    A Maria wants a job. She would like to buy a new bike tire and a new mitt. She talks to her parents. Maria puts up signs.
    B Maria takes the back way home from school. Her bike tire keeps going flat. Maria decided to go a different way home.
    C Maria's bicycle needs fixing. She tells her parents that she will get a job to buy a new tire. They wonder if she will be able to handle the work.
    D Maria's bicycle tire keeps going flat. She wants to get a job to make enough money to buy a new tire. She goes to work at her father's shop.

(Category 2 – 16 – SS)

7 The picture is included in this story to

    A provide information about one of the jobs Maria is willing to do.
    B show one of the chores that Maria does around her home.
    C show how Maria helps her coach set up for ball practice.
    D explain what Maria does after ball practice on Friday.

Read the article "Beavers" before answering the questions below.

My Notes About What I Am Reading

BEAVERS

1. A quiet ripple spreads across the smooth surface of the tree-shaded pond. A furry dark brown head bobs slowly up and down in the water. It is soon joined by five <u>similar</u> shapes. They all belong to the same beaver family. Silently, they glide through the water toward the far side of the pond. The ground slopes down to the pond. The beavers climb out and head to a group of small trees. Each beaver sets to work, cutting down a different tree using its very sharp teeth. Then they cut the trees into smaller pieces and take them back to the water.

2. Beavers make their home mostly in the wooded areas of North America. Forests cover many parts of the United States and Canada. One male and female beaver pick a spot along a small stream or river to build a dam. The dam stops the water from flowing. It backs up forming a pond. This becomes the beavers' home. A house, called a "lodge", is built in the pond.

3. To build their lodge, the beavers cut down many trees. Trees have many different sizes of branches. The beavers put tree branches and rocks into a big pile. This pile can sometimes stick high up out of the water. The beavers use mud to hold everything together.

4. Once the pile is big enough, the beavers will work on the inside. They dive under the water and chew at least two tunnels into the pile. The beavers hollow out the inside of the lodge to make a large room. Here they stay warm, dry, and safe from any enemies.

5. Beavers seem to be the busiest animals in the world. They are always working. They are either building or repairing their lodge or the dam. The hardworking mammals also cut down trees to store as food for the long winter months.

6. Beavers have large webbed back feet. It is difficult for them to move around on land. In the water, however, they are excellent swimmers. Their wide flat tails help steer them swiftly through the water. Beavers can stay underwater for quite a while. Large lungs can hold enough air to let them be under the water for five minutes or longer.

7. Beaver families have one to four babies each year. Young beavers live with their parents for up to two years. During this time, the

parents teach the young beavers what they will need to know to live on their own.

8   Beavers have thick layers of fur to keep them warm and dry. The fur can be different beautiful shades of brown. They keep their fur clean by combing it out with their claws. Beavers make a special oil that they spread all over their fur. This helps keep water away from their bodies. Beavers are able to stay warm and dry no matter how long they are underwater.

9   Beaver parents will live in the same lodge until they die if there are enough trees nearby. They will raise their families in peace and quiet. Working together the beavers will keep their homes safe and free from harm.

My Notes About What I Am Reading

(Category 3 – Figure 19 E – RS)

1   Which of the following is the best summary of the story?

   A   Beavers live where there are many trees. They use them to build a dam across streams or rivers and to make a home. This home is safe and dry in the winter.
   B   Beavers never seem to stop working. They raise their young in a warm and dry home. Beavers cut down trees with their very sharp teeth and move the branches to their lodge.
   C   Beavers build dams on rivers or ponds. They make a home of tree branches and mud where they live and raise their families. Beavers are hardworking animals with bodies that help them work in cold, wet places.
   D   Beavers are able to stay underwater for a long time. They build their lodge near the dam they made to stop the river or stream water from flowing. Special oil keeps the beavers from getting cold and wet.

(Category 1 – 4 C – SS)

2   Which word from paragraph 1 means the opposite of similar?

    A   Dark
    B   Different
    C   Quiet
    D   Small

(Category 3 – Figure 19 D – RS)

3   The author most likely wrote this article to

    A   explain how a dam is made.
    B   describe an animal of the forest.
    C   tell about streams and rivers.
    D   show different animal families of North America.

(Category 3 – 13 C – RS)

4   Beavers are able to stay dry because they

    A   have an oil that covers their body.
    B   have wide flat tails.
    C   have webbed feet that helps them swim.
    D   have sharp teeth.

(Category 3 – Figure 19 D – RS)

5 Which sentence from the passage shows that the beaver mother and father stay together for life?

    A To build their lodge, the beavers cut down many trees.
    B One male and one female beaver pick a spot along a small stream or river to build a dam.
    C Beaver parents will live in the same lodge until they die if there are enough trees nearby.
    D Working together the beavers will keep their homes safe and free from harm.

(Category 3 – 13 A – RS)

6 Which detail sentence from the passage is important to the main idea of the passage?

    A Forests cover many parts of the United States and Canada.
    B The ground slopes down to the pond.
    C To build their lodge, the beavers cut down many trees.
    D Trees have many different sizes of branches.

(Category 3 – 16 – SS)

7 The picture is included in this selection to

    A provide information about what a beaver dam looks like in water.
    B show how a beaver lives in a beaver dam.
    C describe why a beaver puts a dam in water.
    D tell the number of beavers that work on a dam.

Read the passage "My Life as a Colonist" before answering the questions below.

MY LIFE AS A COLONIST

1   I was born in 1735. I lived in Boston, Massachusetts. My father was a silversmith. He <u>created</u> things out of silver. My father made teapots, spoons, cups, and candle sticks. I learned to make them as well.

2   "Paul, take care with every piece that you make," said my father. "Each one is special. It is being made for a valued customer. The customer deserves the best work that you can do."

3   "Yes, father," I replied. "I will remember this."

4   I learned how to be a silversmith. When my father died, I took over the business. In my early twenties, I married Sarah Orne and we had six children. When she died, I married Rachel Walker and had five more children. I took on many other jobs to bring in more money. I made picture frames, rang church bells, made hymn-books, and even became a dentist. I had to work hard to support my family.

5   Massachusetts was a part of England during this time. The government of England began to make the people of Massachusetts and the other colonies in America pay extra money, called" taxes", on many goods. They included newspapers, glass, and tea. England did this without allowing the colonists to help decide what would be taxed and how much. The English government also began to pass other laws without the colonists' vote. This upset many of the people in the American colonies, including me.

6   I joined with other colonists to make problems for the English. One night in December 1773, we dumped three shiploads of tea into the Boston harbor. When we were done, I rode a horse to Philadelphia and New York City, telling them about what had been done to the tea. I became a messenger for the colonists. I was always in danger of being caught by English soldiers.

7   Then one night in April 1775, I was asked to ride from Boston to Concord, Massachusetts. I was to warn other colonists that English troops were on their way. The soldiers were going to Concord to get supplies the colonists had stored in the town.

8   "Please ready my horse," I said to the man at my side. "I must ride and warn the others. I hope I can get to them in time. The people of Concord and other towns need to be ready and safe."

9   "What will you do?" asked the man as he saddled my horse.

My Notes About What I Am Reading

10 "I will see one lit lantern in the tower of the church if the English are moving by land and two lanterns if they are moving by water," I replied. I looked out at the tower. I saw how the English were moving.

11 I jumped on a waiting horse and took off for Concord. Some English soldiers tried to stop me along the way, but I got away from them. I rode on to Lexington and warned the colonists in the town. Moving on, I was captured by English soldiers not far outside of Lexington. They let me go. I had to <u>abandon</u> my horse and go back without it. I did not reach Concord, but other messengers had managed to tell the town that the soldiers were coming. They were ready for the English. A fierce battle was fought at Concord. The English troops finally gave up and returned to Boston. The war had started.

12 I continued to be a messenger. I also printed money, made cannons, and was in charge of a fort near Boston.

13 When the war was over, I returned to being a silversmith. Later, I had a hardware store and ran a foundry where I made stoves, church bells, and other things out of metal. I enjoyed my life in Boston.

My Notes About What I Am Reading

(Category 1 – 4 B – RS)

1 Which word in paragraphs 1 or 2 help the reader know what <u>created</u> means?

A Lived
B Learned
C Made
D Took

(Category 2 – 9 – SS)

2 The information included in "My Life as a Colonist" helps the reader better understand Paul Revere by

   A explaining to the reader how work can change people's lives.
   B describing what Paul Revere did to help his country.
   C showing what Paul Revere did when he worked for his father.
   D telling the reader about being a silversmith.

(Category 2 – Figure 19 D – SS)

3 The reader can tell from the passage that

   A Paul's father worked long hours.
   B Paul's father cares about him.
   C Paul is surprised about his father.
   D Paul is angry at his father.

(Category 2 – Figure 19 E – SS)

4 Which is the best summary of the passage?

   A Paul Revere rides a horse to warn people in towns near Boston that English soldiers are coming. Some of the English soldiers try to stop him. They take his horse so Paul is not able to warn the people. Other people are able to tell the towns.
   B Paul Revere learns to be a silversmith. He is able to make many useful things out of silver. His father shows him what to do to help make customers happy. Paul tells his father that he will remember to do this while he is a silversmith.
   C Paul Revere watches for English soldiers. He wants to warn other people who live nearby that the soldiers are coming. Paul sees two lit lanterns in the tall tower of a church in Boston. This shows that the soldiers are moving by water.
   D Paul Revere grows up in Boston where his father is a silversmith. Paul learns to be a silversmith, too. Joining with other people, Paul works to get rid of the English that rule the land. He tries to tell other people that English soldiers are coming but gets stopped.

(Category 1 – 4 B – RS)

5 In paragraph 11, the word <u>abandon</u> means

    A leave.
    B feed.
    C rest.
    D carry.

(Category 2 – Figure 19 D – SS)

6 From information in the passage, how does Paul feel about the people in Concord?

    A Jealous
    B Disappointed
    C Worried
    D Sad

Read the story "Which Plant Will Grow the Tallest?" before answering the questions below.

	My Notes About What I Am Reading

WHICH PLANT WILL GROW THE TALLEST?

1. "Mom, the science fair is next month and I don't have any idea what to do," Natalie whined as she climbed into the car. "By tomorrow's science class, Mrs. Gordon wants us to tell her what our projects are going to be about. I have been thinking all week and I haven't come up with a thing. I have lots of math homework to do, but it does not have to be turned in until later in the week."

2. "Well, Natalie, why don't we go to the plant store? Maybe you can think of an idea for the science fair there. Besides, I want to get some tomato plants for our pot garden," said Mom.

3. "Judy and Frank are already doing theirs on plants and light," replied Natalie. "What else is there?"

4. Mom drove on to the plant store. Natalie and her mom found the tomato plants and pots they wanted for their pot garden. Next to the checkout stand was a bookcase full of books about plants. Mom noticed a book titled "Science Fair Projects with Plants." The book explained different experiments that can be done using plants.

5. "This looks like a book that might help you decide on a project," Mom said. She put it with the tomato plants and stood in line to check out.

6. Back in the car, Natalie pulled the book out of one of the sacks. She began to read it. After reading a while, Natalie looked at her mom and said, "I think I found a project. Listen to this and see what you think, Mom. This is kind of long, but I can't wait."

Does Soil Make a Difference?

Here is what you will need:

 3 - six-inch clay pots with a drain hole in the bottom
 3 - drain plates, one for each clay pot
 12 - bean seeds
 30 - rocks the size of grapes
 1 - thirty-two-ounce measuring cup
 1 - twelve-inch ruler
 1 - Plant Growth Chart

You will also need enough of each of the following kinds of soils to fill a six-inch clay pot:

>sand
>potting soil
>soil from around your home

Here is what you will need to do:

1. Place each six-inch clay pot on its drain plate.

2. Put eight to ten grape-size rocks in the bottom of each pot.

3. Fill one pot with sand, another with potting soil, and the third with soil found around your home.

4. Push four bean seeds one inch deep into each pot. Cover the seeds with the soil from the pot.

5. Using the measuring cup, pour eight ounces of water into each pot.

6. Write the date the seeds were planted for each kind of soil on the "Plant Growth Chart."

7. Put the three pots on a windowsill that receives sunlight during the day.

8. Check the three pots each day. Do this at the same time. Watch to see when the bean plants first break out of the soil. Write this date on the "Plant Growth Chart."

9. Continue to water each plant every other day with three or four ounces of water. If you need to water less often, treat each plant the same. Water them the same amount of water and all three at the same time.

10. When the first plant pops out of the soil, measure how tall it is from the top of the clay pot to the top of the plant. Write this on the chart. If the other pots have no plants, write a zero. If a pot has more than one plant out of the soil, measure the tallest.

11. Observe the three pots for fourteen days after the first plant comes up. Remember to water all three pots with the same amount of water and at the same time. Also, keep the three pots in the same amount of sunlight. At the end of the two weeks, decide which soil grew the tallest plant.

7 Mom pulled into the driveway as Natalie finished reading from the book. Natalie turned the page while her mom drove into the garage and shut off the car. Mom leaned over to take a <u>glimpse</u> of the page that Natalie had turned to in the book. "Let me have a look at that page," Mom said.

My Notes About What I Am Reading

8 "Here is the plant sheet," said Natalie. "It shows the question to find out about and the hypothesis. It also has the chart to fill in during the experiment. I think this is going to work. What do you think, Mom?"

9 "I think you have found your project for the science fair. What do you say we go back to the plant store and get what you need? We've got an hour before your father gets home from work," answered Mom.

My Notes About What I Am Reading

Plant Growth

Question: Which kind of soil will grow the tallest bean plant?

Hypothesis: (This is a guess of what you think will happen. Circle which soil you think will grow the tallest bean plants. After the experiment you will be able to see if you were right or not.)

I think the bean grown in

sand / potting soil / my soil

will grow the tallest.

Data:

	Date Seeds Planted	Date Seeds Come Up	Date and How tall in inches	Date and How tall in inches	Date and How tall in inches	Date and How tall in inches	Date and How tall in inches	Date and How tall in inches	Date and How tall in inches
Plant in Sand									
Plant in Potting Soil									
Plant in Your Soil									

Conclusion: (Circle if you were right or not right about your hypothesis.)

I was

right / not right

about which soil will grow the tallest bean plant.

This is what I learned from my experiment:

_____
_____
_____
_____
_____
_____

My Notes About What I Am Reading

(Category 1 – 4 B – RS)

1 In paragraph 7, which word helps the reader know what <u>glimpse</u> means?

  A Drove
  B Look
  C Pulled
  D Turned

(Category 3 – 13 D – RS)

2 Which section of "Plant Growth" will give Natalie information about how tall the plants get that she plants for the science fair?

  A Question
  B Hypothesis
  C Data
  D Conclusion

(Category 2 – Figure 19 D – RS)

3 What will Natalie probably do before her dad comes home from work?

    A Work on her idea for the science fair.
    B Plant tomato plants in pots.
    C Finish her math homework.
    D Call her friends to talk about their science fair idea.

(Category 2 – 2 B – SS)

4 After telling her mom about the science fair, Natalie goes to the plant store to

    A talk with Judy and Frank.
    B buy a book about tomatoes.
    C talk to her father about the science fair.
    D look for an idea for the science fair.

(Category 2 – Figure 19 E – RS)

5 Read the first sentence of the summary below to answer the next question.

> **Summary of "Which Plant Will Grow the Tallest?"**
> Natalie needs to think of something to do for the science fair.

Which sentences complete the summary?

    A She worries about what to do for the science fair. Her mother gets plants from a plant store. Natalie helps her get them home.
    B She goes to a plant store to get some plants. Then she goes home. Natalie waits there for her father to arrive.
    C She goes with her mother to a plant store. There she gets a book with ideas of what to do at a science fair. Natalie picks something to do.
    D She helps her mother pick out plants for their family garden at a plant store. Then they go home to put the plants into pots.

(Category 3 – 13 D – RS)

6 Which part of "Does Soil Make a Difference?" gives information about when to water the plants?

  A   Part 3
  B   Part 5
  C   Part 7
  D   Part 9

(Category 3 – 15 B – SS)

7 The chart is included in this passage to help the reader

  A   understand what information is being recorded for the science fair.
  B   know what the plants will do for the science fair.
  C   learn where a plant grows.
  D   identify the tools used for the science fair.

Read the story "The Big Brother" before answering the questions below.

THE BIG BROTHER

1. Analina knocked on her older brother's bedroom door. She knew if his door was closed he usually did not want to be bothered. Nevertheless, Analina needed his help. Her class was learning about animals. The students had been put in groups. Each group was to show the rest of the class what they had learned. Analina's group had studied about animals that live in jungles and rain forests. The students of her group decided to make masks of the different animals. Analina had learned about leopards.

2. Two weeks ago, Analina had found a book at the school library on making animal masks. She checked it out after looking in its table of contents. Chapter two was about how to make masks of lions, tigers, cheetahs, and leopards. Analina had brought the book home right away, but put it aside. Her report—which included all she had learned about her animal—took most of her time.

3. The masks were to be finished by tomorrow. When she had gone to the book to make her mask, she found one of the pages of directions missing. Only half of the directions were there. Analina did not know what to do. She thought her brother might know what to do.

4. Analina knocked on the door, harder this time.

5. "Yes? Come in," her brother said.

6. "I am sorry to bother you, but I need your help," Analina said.

7. "Ana, you are not a bother," replied Nick. "What help do you need from me?"

8. Analina explained to Nick about the mask and the book. When she had finished, he smiled and said to her, "I remember when we made animal masks when I was at your school. It was fun. In fact, I think we used the same book. But there were no pages missing when we checked it out. I think I know where we can look."

9. Nick turned in his chair and started typing on his computer keyboard. In a moment, he looked up at the screen with a big grin on his face.

10. "Here Ana, look at this," said Nick turning the screen so she could see.

11. Analina saw a picture of a beautiful, spotted animal. The leopard's eyes were coals in a roaring fire. A colorful mask was also pictured.

My Notes About What I Am Reading

The picture took up only one corner while directions on how to make the mask took up the rest of the screen.

12 "Do you think you will be able to make this mask from these directions?" Nick asked.

13 "Wow! This is great! Let me read them to see," exclaimed Analina. She read through the directions. Nick waited patiently.

14 "I am pretty sure that I can make a leopard mask from the directions," Analina said after a couple of minutes. "I have all of the paper, paint, sack, and other things to make the mask with here at home."

15 "Okay, I'll just print these out and you can get started," said Nick.

16 "Thanks, Nick," said Analina.

17 "No problem," answered Nick. "That's what big brothers are for, aren't they?"

Leopard Mask

1. To make a leopard mask you will need:

   1 large paper grocery sack

   1 small bottle of yellow tempera paint

   1 small bottle of black tempera paint

   1 small paint brush

   2 bowls to hold the two colors of paint

   1 bowl to hold water to clean the paint brush

   1 roll of paper towels

   1 nine-inch-by-twelve-inch piece of black construction paper

   2 twelve-inch pieces of string

   1 bottle of white glue

   1 pair of scissors

   1 twelve-inch ruler

My Notes About What I Am Reading

2. Turn the grocery sack upside down. Cut an opening for your eyes in the front and middle of the sack about three inches from the bottom. Make it in the shape of a rectangle.

3. Cut out two ears for the leopard from the black construction paper. Glue them onto the paper sack.

4. Paint the outside of the entire sack with the yellow paint. Let it dry.

5. Paint small black spots all over the mask with the black tempera paint.

6. Paint one black eye on each side of the eye opening. Paint a round nose with the black paint in the middle of the sack under the eye opening.

7. Paint a mouth with the black paint under the nose.

8. Cut out six to eight long thin strips of black construction paper for the whiskers. Glue three to four strips on each side of the nose.

9. Let everything dry overnight.

My Notes About What I Am Reading

(Category 2 – 2 B – SS)

1. What is Analina's main problem in the story?

    A   She had to make a leopard mask by tomorrow.
    B   She had to finish writing what she had learned about leopards.
    C   She had to get the things she needed to make the leopard mask.
    D   She had to check out books about leopards from the library.

(Category 2 – 8 B – RS)

2. How does Nick feel about helping with Analina's problem?

    A   Angry
    B   Caring
    C   Excited
    D   Lazy

(Category 2 – 8 A – RS)

3   The events in the story took place at Analina's house. Why is this important?

   A   Analina looks for directions about a leopard mask.
   B   Analina is able to make her mask for her school group.
   C   Analina is able to finish writing about leopards.
   D   Analina is able to turn to her brother for help.

(Category 2 – 5 A – SS)

4   What is the theme of the story?

   A   Keep your brother happy
   B   Never be afraid to ask for help
   C   Finish work early
   D   Learn about animals

(Category 2 – Figure 19 D – RS)

5   Which sentence from the story shows that Analina was worried about asking Nick for help?

   A   "I'm sorry to bother you, but I need your help."
   B   "I am pretty sure that I can make a leopard mask from the directions"
   C   She read through the directions.
   D   She thought her older brother would know what to do.

(Category 3 – 15 B – SS)

6   Below is a list of steps Analina followed when she made the leopard mask.

> 1. Analina cut out an opening for her eyes.
> 2. Analina glued two ears on the sack.
> 3. _____
> 4. Analina put black spots on the mask.

Which of these belongs beside the number 3?

A   Analina cut out thin strips of black paper.
B   Analina painted the sack yellow.
C   Analina put a nose in the middle of the sack.
D   Analina painted a mouth at the bottom.

(Category 2 – 10 A – SS)

7   Read this sentence from the passage.

> **The leopard's eyes were coals in a roaring fire.**

The author uses these words to

A   tell what the leopard was doing.
B   explain why Analina wants to make a leopard mask.
C   describe how Analina saw the leopard's eyes.
D   show where the leopard's eyes were looking.

Read the story "The Bake Sale" before answering the questions below.

THE BAKE SALE

My Notes About What I Am Reading

1   "We need only $100 more to buy the new slide for our neighborhood playground," Mr. Johnson said. "Does anyone have any suggestions on how we can raise the money?"

2   The monthly meeting of The Meadows neighborhood group was about over. This was the last thing to be decided. No one said a word. All was quiet. Then Mr. Jenkins said, "We've had car washes, carnivals, fun runs, raffles, and sold T-shirts. What's left to do?"

3   "How about a bake sale?" said a small voice in the back of the room. All eyes turned to find out who had made the suggestion. "Everyone in the neighborhood can bring something and we can sell the food next Saturday at the town picnic," said Veronica, the owner of the small voice. "There will be a lot people there for the five-mile race."

4   "That sounds like a wonderful idea, Veronica," said Ms. Timmerman. "I can bake my delicious chocolate cake. We can sell it by the slice."

5   "Yeah, and I can make some apple pies," added Beth. "I sprinkle some cinnamon on top. It tastes real good with a scoop of vanilla ice cream."

6   Arthur jumped out of his chair and exclaimed, "I can make some chocolate chip cookies! I learned how at my cooking class last summer. I know people will like them. I can't stop eating them myself!"

7   Everyone started talking at once. Each of the neighbors offered to bake one or more things for the bake sale. Mr. Johnson wrote all of the names in his notebook.

8   "How are we going to let the town know about our bake sale?" Mr. Johnson asked as he finished with the names.

9   "Should we make a flyer telling about the sale?" suggested Veronica.

10   "Sounds like another good idea, Veronica," said Ms. Timmerman. "Do you think you could make a flyer for us? If you get one ready, my shop will print enough copies to go all over town."

11   "Sure, I can do that," replied Veronica. "Let me work on it tomorrow. I have to be in my class play at school in the morning, but I will have enough of the day left to run it over to you by 3:00 p.m. This should give you plenty of time to print the copies. My friends and I will also

help <u>distribute</u> them. We can give them out around the neighborhood."

12 Mr. Johnson stood up and said, "We all have our jobs to do. This meeting is finished. We will see you all next Saturday."

13 Veronica worked on the flyer the next day. She finally got it the way she wanted it to look. Then she took it to Ms. Timmerman's print shop.

14 "Here is the flyer," said Veronica as she walked into Ms. Timmerman's shop.

15 "Wow!" Ms. Timmerman said as she read the flyer. "It looks great. All of the information is here to let the town know all about the bake sale. I will print this right up. The copies should be ready by late afternoon. That will give us lots of time to hand them out. Veronica, I was not sure about you and your friends at the start of our group's work on getting a new playground. However, you and your friends have done well. I would like to thank you for giving us an idea on how to raise the last bit of money needed for our slide. Your help with making and handing out the flyer will make sure that our goal is met."

16 "You are welcome," answered Veronica. "I can't wait to play on that new slide."

Bake Sale for New Slide!

Who: The Meadows Neighborhood Group
What: Bake Sale
When: Saturday, April 10 – 11:00 a.m. – 3:00 p.m.
Where: The Town Picnic at City Park
Why: To raise money for a slide to go onto the Meadows Neighborhood playground

---

Here are some things that will be for sale:

- **Chocolate Cake by the Slice**
- **Apple Pie with Cinnamon**
- **Homemade Ice Cream**
- **Chocolate Chip Cookies**
- **Fudge Brownies**
- **Peach Cobbler**
- **Pumpkin Pie**
- **Peanut Butter Cookies**
- **Angel Food Cake**

- *Buy a dessert to go with your picnic lunch!*
- *After you play that hot baseball game, come get some ice cream!*
- *A homemade piece of cake goes great with the checkers contest!*
- *Help support our new playground!*

My Notes About What I Am Reading

(Category 2 – Figure 19 E – RS)

1 Which of these gives the best summary of the story?

   A The Meadows neighborhood group decides to have a bake sale. Veronica gets people to make food for the sale. They will bring their food to the park for the town picnic.

   B Ms. Timmerman says she will print flyers for a neighborhood bake sale. Many neighbors say they will help bake food for the sale. Veronica and her friends will hand out the flyers.

   C The Meadows neighborhood group needs to raise money for a playground slide. Veronica thinks of a bake sale. Many people say they will help. Veronica makes a flyer telling all about the sale.

   D Mr. Johnson leads a meeting for a neighborhood group. He writes down the names of people who say they will help with a bake sale. Veronica will work on a flyer about the sale in time for the town picnic.

(Category 2 – 2 B – SS)

2 What is the main problem in the story?

   A Veronica has to make a flyer before the town picnic.
   B Veronica has to find a way to hand out flyers for a bake sale.
   C A group of neighbors needs to decide what to have for a bake sale.
   D A group of neighbors needs to raise enough money to buy a playground slide.

(Category 1 – 4 C – SS)

3   In paragraph 11, which word means about the same as <u>distribute</u>?

   A   Give
   B   Help
   C   Run
   D   Work

(Category 2 – 8 B – RS)

4   How does Arthur feel about being able to bring something to the bake sale?

   A   Angry
   B   Excited
   C   Foolish
   D   Surprised

(Category 2 – 8 B – RS)

5   How does Ms. Timmerman feel about Veronica's help with raising money for the playground?

   A   At first, Ms. Timmerman is worried, but now she is thankful.
   B   At first, Ms. Timmerman is excited but now she is unsure.
   C   At first, Ms. Timmerman is proud, but now she is bothered.
   D   At first, Ms. Timmerman is disappointed, but now she is surprised.

(Category 3 – 15 B – SS)

6 Look at the chart below. It shows what events were going to take place at the town picnic.

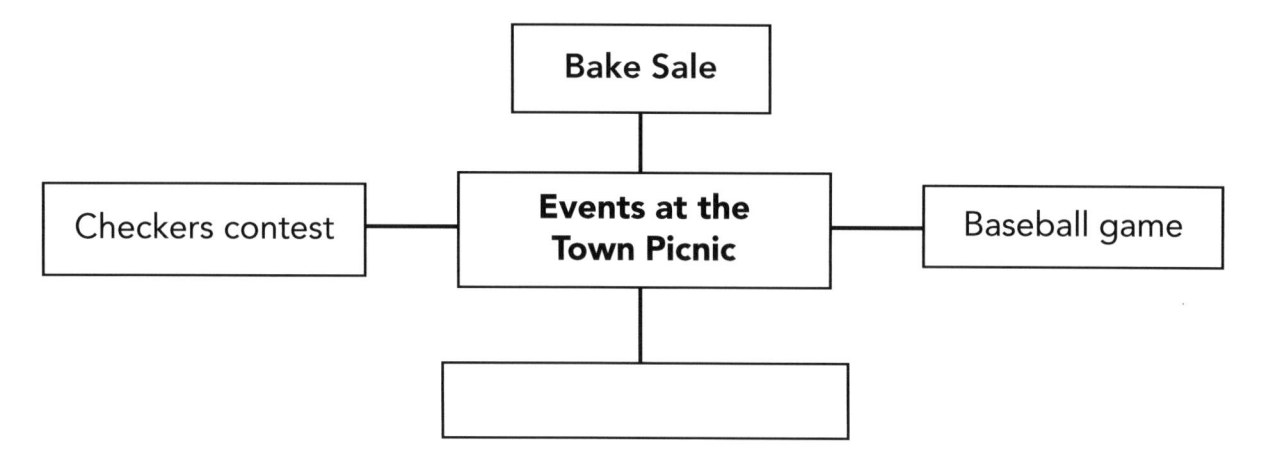

```
                    ┌─────────────┐
                    │  Bake Sale  │
                    └──────┬──────┘
                           │
┌──────────────────┐   ┌───┴──────────────┐   ┌───────────────┐
│ Checkers contest │───│  Events at the   │───│ Baseball game │
└──────────────────┘   │   Town Picnic    │   └───────────────┘
                       └───────┬──────────┘
                               │
                       ┌───────┴──────────┐
                       │                  │
                       └──────────────────┘
```

Which event belongs in the empty box?

A   Car wash
B   Cooking class
C   Five-mile race
D   Class play at school

(Category 2 – 16 – SS)

7 Why does the author include the picture with the passage?

   A   To show where the bake sale is to be held
   B   To give information about what the money raised will buy
   C   To explain what will be sold at the bake sale
   D   To show who will come and be working at the bake sale

Read the poem "Lazy Dog" before answering the questions below.

LAZY DOG

I have a dog and would you believe,
He's a bear. He's a horse.

He is so slow and lazy,
He could never catch a cat, of course.

He spends his days as a mouse,
No noise, not even a peep.

At night he climbs into my bed,
And there he will go to sleep.

He likes to watch me play at times,
As long as he is still.

He looks like he might get up,
But I don't think he will.

He often looks around,
And opens his mouth in a yawn.

Then he stretches out for a nice long nap,
Content to snooze in a patch of lawn.

My Notes About What I Am Reading

(Category 1 – 4 B – RS)

1 Which meaning best fits the way <u>patch</u> is used in line 16?

    A A piece of material
    B To put on
    C A spot
    D To fix quickly

(Category 2 – 2 B – SS)

2 What does the dog do in the sun?

    A Look for food
    B Take a nap
    C Watch someone play
    D Catch a cat

(Category 1 – 4 B – RS)

3 What does <u>content</u> mean in line 16?

    A Happy
    B What is inside
    C Meaning
    D What is in a book

(Category 2 – 6 A – SS)

4 Which words from the poem help the reader make a picture of the size of the dog?

    A Even a peep
    B Nice long nap
    C He often looks around
    D He's a horse

Category 2 – 6 A – SS)

5 What kind of poetry is "Lazy Dog"?

    A Free verse
    B Humorous
    C Lyrical
    D Narrative

(Category 2 – 6 A – SS)

6 Read this line from the poem.

> **He spends his days as a mouse,**

The poet includes this line most likely to show the dog is

A quiet.
B quick.
C tired.
D hungry.

Category 2 – 6 A – SS)

7 Lines 1 and 2 are important to the poem because they show that the dog

A is a big size.
B can move quickly.
C is a friendly animal.
D can make friends.

Read the passage "Benjamin Franklin's Journal" before answering the questions below.

If Benjamin Franklin had kept a journal, here are a few things he may have written about his life.

BENJAMIN FRANKLIN'S JOURNAL

July 12

1   The boy could not believe what he was seeing! A kite was pulling me across the pond! I was holding tightly to the end of the string attached to the kite. The wind pushed the kite toward the other side of the pond. I just hung on and let the kite do all of the work. These ideas just seem to come to me.

January 17

2   I was born on this day in 1706. I live when the colonies are a part of England.

3   I was born in Boston, Massachusetts. My father is a candle maker. I have many brothers and sisters. They all help with the many jobs of a candle shop. I like to learn about things. I am always trying something different.

April 2

4   I quit school today. I am now 12 years old. I am going to work for my older brother, James. James is a printer. He prints a newspaper.

March 15

5   I have been working many long hours for my brother. It has been seven years since I started working for him. I have learned much about the printing and newspaper business. I also have begun to write. I have written poems, stories, letters, and newspaper articles. When I am not writing, I am reading.

6   But I do not want to stay working for my brother much longer. I have many ideas that I want to try.

October 10

7   I have left my brother in Boston and moved to Philadelphia to <u>seek</u> a new life. I have found a job working for another printer. I have been working hard for my money. I have enough to have my own printing business.

June 12

8   I am married and have children. My print shop has done well. I have started a successful newspaper. I also have written and pub-

My Notes About What I Am Reading

lished a book called *Poor Richard's Almanack*. It is full of all sorts of information. It has a calendar, maps, and information about the weather. Many people have bought this book.

9   I am also helping my city become a better place to live. I have started the first library where people can check out books for free. I have started a fire department. I helped start a hospital and a school in this city.

August 3

10 I am now forty-two years old. I have left my printing business. I have enough money for my family to live well. I am spending time inventing things. I have been quite busy as an inventor. I invented a stove made of iron. It gives off more heat than other stoves and cost less to use. I invented a clock that shows the hours, minutes, and the seconds. I invented the lightning rod to protect buildings from lightning strikes. I also invented bifocal glasses. These glasses have two lenses in one frame. They help people see things both far away and close up clearly.

February 11

11 I have tried to make this country a better place to live. I have found ways to send mail faster and safer. I have been to England to speak to the government there. I tried to help them see that the people back in America want to live well and safely. But the government in England makes this hard for the people in America. It is the year 1775. It is time to return home to my land of America.

June 23

12 I believe that America needs to be free from England. I want to help make this happen. I have worked on writing the Declaration of Independence for our colonies. We are now at war with England to win our freedom. I have gone to France to ask for their help. France has agreed. With their help, we can defeat England.

May 10

13 The war with England is over. I am helping to write the Constitution of the United States. It will be a great document for our country.

My Notes About What I Am Reading

Time Line of My Life

1706	Born in Boston, Massachusetts.
1716	Work in my father's candle shop.
1718	Go to work to learn to be a printer with my older brother.
1723	Go to Philadelphia.
1728	Starts my own printing business.
1730	Marry Deborah Read. A child, William, is born.
1732	Poor Richard's Almanack is first published.
1743	A child, Sarah, is born.
1744	Invent my iron stove.
1748	Leave my printing business.
1752	Invent the lightning rod.
1757	Go to England.
1775	Return to America. War between America and England breaks out.
1776	Sail to France to ask for their help in the war.
1783	The war ends. Help America and England work things out.
1784	Invent glasses to help people see better.
1785	Return to America.
1787	Help write the Constitution of the United States.

My Notes About What I Am Reading

(Category 2 – Figure 19 E – SS)

1   Read the first two sentences of a summary of the passage.

> **Summary**
> Benjamin Franklin learned to be a printer and had a printing shop of his own. He made many useful things to help people live better lives.
> _____
> _____

Which sentence best completes the summary?

A   Benjamin Franklin served his country and helped it become free.
B   Benjamin Franklin went to France to ask for help in the war against England.
C   Benjamin Franklin made a new stove and special glasses to help people see better.
D   Benjamin Franklin helped his country write new laws.

(Category 2 – 2 B – SS)

2 Using the timeline, what happened to Benjamin Franklin?

   A   He had many children.
   B   He was born in Philadelphia.
   C   He lived some of his life in England.
   D   He worked as a printer all of his life.

(Category 2 – Figure 19 D – SS)

3 Which sentence from the passage tells the reader that Benjamin Franklin took care of his money?

   A   I like to learn about things.
   B   I am always trying something different.
   C   I have enough to have my own printing business.
   D   I am also helping my city become a better place to live.

(Category 2 – 2 B – SS)

4 Benjamin Franklin went to France to

   A   ask its help to be free from England.
   B   study about its way of making glasses.
   C   start a printing business.
   D   work on a newspaper.

(Category 1 – 4 B – RS)

5 What does the word <u>seek</u> mean in paragraph 7?

A Decide
B Look for
C Spend
D Trade

Read the poem "The Wind" before answering the questions below.

THE WIND

It is soft and cooling all around,
When the heat comes from above.
It picks up leaves and spins them to the ground,
4   With a push and then a shove.

When the clouds are dark and gray,
It's there and you will see.
Come the night and come the day,
8   It can lift an old oak tree.

It quietly lifts a bright blue feather,
Way up into the sky.
No matter what the time or the weather,
12   So just say good-bye.

As known as a dear old friend,
It's like an old worn hat.
It never seems to end
16   Not sure of what I think of that.

Though the sky be oh, so clear,
It is quite plain to me.
It moves without any fear,
20   The wind is wild and free.

My Notes About What I Am Reading

(Category 2 – 6 A – SS)

1. "The Wind" is an example of which kind of poetry?

   A Free verse
   B Humorous
   C Lyrical
   D Narrative

(Category 2 – 2 B – SS)

2. What does the wind do to the feather?

   A Spins it
   B Lifts it
   C Pushes it
   D Cools it

(Category 1 – 4 B – RS)

3. Which meaning best fits the way <u>clear</u> is used in stanza 5?

   A Free from clouds
   B Easily seen
   C Certain
   D Free from needing to pay money

(Category 1 – 4 B – RS)

4 Which meaning of <u>free</u> best fits the way the word is used in stanza 5?

    A Willing to share
    B Not having to be right
    C Not having to follow the rules
    D Able to go anywhere

(Category 2 – Figure 19 E – SS)

5 Which is the best summary of the poem "The Wind"?

    A The wind blows leaves. It is strong and can lift trees. The wind comes during the day.
    B The wind lifts things. It blows things around. The wind moves.
    C The wind is able to lift light and heavy things. It can blow at any time. The wind can go anywhere.
    D The wind is like a friend. It can cool things off. The wind is able to go here and there.

(Category 2 – Figure 19 D – SS)

6 What can the reader tell about the wind in the poem?

    A It is always safe.
    B It is always around.
    C It is always weak.
    D It is always soft.

(Category 2 – 2 B – SS)

7 What is the speaker doing in the poem?

   A   watching the wind.
   B   playing in the wind.
   C   ignoring the wind.
   D   talking to the wind.

(Category 2 – 6 A – SS)

8 Lines 5 through 8 are included in the poem because they

   A   list reasons the wind blows.
   B   give examples of how the wind is friendly.
   C   explain why the wind is cooling.
   D   tell how the wind is strong.

Read the story "Someone to Count On" before answering the questions below.

My Notes About What I Am Reading

SOMEONE TO COUNT ON

1 "Maybe I can use the directions for making those chocolate chip cookies that are on the back of the chocolate bag?" Max wondered out loud. "No, that has too much sugar in it."

2 Max was sprawled out across his bed. It was Spring Break. He was trying to come up with a recipe for the class cookbook. Each year the third grade at Emerson Elementary School made a cookbook. Every recipe he thought of was already being used by someone else or was too sweet.

3 Max rolled over and peered out of his bedroom window. He watched his mom as she made the flower bed <u>clean</u>. She wanted to get rid of everything and plant roses. Max saw a car turn into his neighbor's driveway. A man got out carrying a big bag with steam streaming out of its sides.

4 "That's it!" hollered Max. "I'll make pizza. I can make it healthy and not sweet!" Max went to the living room and grabbed the telephone. He wanted to call his friend Jack and see if Jack knew of a good recipe for pizza. Jack's mom, Mrs. Anderson, answered the phone. She told Max that Jack was visiting his grandparents in another city. Mrs. Anderson said that she would have Jack get in touch with him. Max thanked her and hung up.

5 "Now I remember," Max said to himself. "He went to visit his grandparents over Spring Break. Jack will be back home on Sunday night. I sure wish I could talk to him."

6 Two days later, Max went to get his family's mail from the mailbox. An envelope with his name on it was at the top of the pile of mail. He opened it. The letter inside was from his friend Jack. Jack had put a set of directions inside on how to make pizza along with a chart telling how many slices to cut different sizes of pizza.

March 16th

Dear Max,

7 *How is it going, buddy? I am having a great time here at my grandparents' house. We have gone fishing every day.*

8 *My mom called and said that you finally thought of a food to make for our cookbook. Yes, I do have a recipe. My grandma helped me come up with one. She took one she had and changed it a little so*

that it would be easier to make. I have written it below. It sure is good.

9   *I will be back home Sunday evening. I'll see you then.*

Your friend,
Jack

Jack's Pepperoni Pizza

Things you will need:

1 – twelve-inch prebaked pizza crust

1 – small can of pizza sauce

8 ounces of grated mozzarella cheese

20 slices of pepperoni

What to do:

1. Preheat the oven to 450 degrees Fahrenheit.

2. Spread the pizza sauce on top of the pizza crust.

3. Put most of the cheese on top of the sauce

4. Put slices of pepperoni evenly all over the top of the cheese.

5. Spread the rest of the cheese over the pepperoni slices.

6. Bake in the oven for eight to ten minutes or until the cheese is melted and has turned light brown in color.

Size of Pizza	Number of Slices
Small	4
Medium	8
Large	12
Extra Large	8

10 Max licked his lips. "This sounds pretty good!" he said.

11 Max grabbed the rest of the mail and headed back to his house. Then he sat down and made a list of what he needed to get at the store to make the pizza. When his mom came in from working in the yard, he explained what he wanted to do.

My Notes About What I Am Reading

12 "That sure was nice of Jack to do this for you," said Mom. "

13 "Yes, it was," said Max. "He is such a good, good friend. He didn't have to do this, but he knew I needed help."

14 "Let's go to the store after lunch," Mom suggested. "You can try the recipe tonight for supper."

My Notes About What I Am Reading

(Category 1 – 4 A – RS)

1 If "heat" means to make hot, what does <u>preheat</u> mean in paragraph 9?

    A Make hot again
    B Make hot before
    C Not make hot
    D Sometimes make hot

(Category 2 – 2 B- SS)

2 What is Max's main problem in the story?

    A He wants to talk with Jack.
    B He needs to clean out the flower bed.
    C He has to wait for his mom to come home.
    D He has to decide on a food to make for the cookbook.

(Category 2 – Figure 19 D – RS)

3   The title of the story is "Someone to Count On". Which sentence from the story shows that the title is true?

   A   Jack will be back home on Sunday night.
   B   Mrs. Anderson said that she would have Jack get in touch with him.
   C   Jack had put a set of directions inside on how to make pizza.
   D   She told Max that Jack was visiting his grandparents in another city.

(Category 1 – 4 B – RS)

4   Which meaning best fits the way <u>clean</u> is used in paragraph 3?
   A   Neat
   B   Have no mistakes
   C   Fair
   D   Clear

(Category 2 – 8 B – RS)

5   When Max gets off of the phone with Mrs. Anderson, he feels

   A   afraid.
   B   angry.
   C   disappointed.
   D   sad.

(Category 2 – 5 A – SS)

6   The theme of this story is

    A   friends help friends.
    B   eat healthy food.
    C   take time to visit family.
    D   be prepared.

(Category 3 – 15 B – SS)

7   Using information found in the passage, which size pizza is cut into 12 slices?

    A   Small
    B   Medium
    C   Large
    D   Extra large

Read the story "Problem Solved" before answering the questions below.

PROBLEM SOLVED

1 "Something keeps eating my tomato plants," Elena complained. She pulled a few more weeds and then sat down next to her dad. He was painting the back porch. "I am afraid that it will eat all of my buds before any of them have a chance to grow into tomatoes. Mrs. Ruiz's plants next door always look so good. I wonder what she does?"

2 "Elena, I know you wanted to do this garden all by yourself. I want to finish painting our porch before your grandparents come for a visit next week. So, may I make a suggestion?" asked Dad.

3 "Yes, please do," answered Elena.

4 "Get some birds to come to your garden," Dad said.

5 "You mean go buy a couple of birds and keep them in a cage out in the garden?" asked Elena.

6 "No, honey," replied Dad. "Make a bird feeder. Get some birds to hang around your garden. They will eat the pests that are feasting on your tomato plants. The whole garden will be better off."

7 "Let's go make one now," Elena said. She jumped up and pulled on her father's hand, trying to get him away from his paintbrush.

8 "Whoa! What ever happened to wanting to do this garden by yourself?" laughed Dad.

9 "I know when I need help. Let's get started before my tomato plants are all gone," exclaimed Elena.

10 Dad set down his paintbrush and walked into the house. Elena followed him. He went into the study and took a book off of one of the many shelves. Quickly flipping pages, he reached down and showed Elena one of the worn pages:

My Notes About What I Am Reading

My Notes About What I Am Reading

Bird Feeder

What You Will Need to Make Your Bird Feeder:
- 1 half-gallon milk or juice carton
- 1 thin and straight stick from a tree, about eighteen inches long
- 4 rocks the size of a golf ball
- 1 pair of pointed scissors
- 1 small nail
- 2 feet of twine or string
  birdseed

How to Make Your Bird Feeder:
1. Wash out the carton well. Let it dry.
2. Cut out a four-inch by six-inch rectangle out of the center of two opposite sides of the carton. Make the openings about one inch down from the top of both sides. This will allow a deep area for the birdseed.
3. Make a hole in each side of the carton about halfway between the bottom and the opening made in step 2. Put the holes on the same sides as the openings. Push the stick through both holes so it sticks out evenly on both sides of the carton. This will be a perch for the birds.
4. Using the nail, put five or six small holes in the bottom of the carton. This is for water to drain out.
5. Put the four rocks in the bottom of the carton.
6. Put a hole at the top in the center of the carton. Put the twine through the hole.
7. Fill the bottom of the carton with the birdseed.
8. Tie the twine or string around a strong branch of a tree. Enjoy watching the birds!

11 "I made this bird feeder when I was about your age," he said. "My dad showed me this feeder when I had the same problem you have. It took me about an hour to make."

12 "Did it work? Did the birds come and eat the pests?" Elena asked.

13 "Just wait and see," Dad replied.

14 Elena took the book from her dad. She read the directions on how to make the bird feeder. Then she gathered all of the things she needed and got to work building her feeder.

15 Elena's dad walked into her room just as she was tying the brown twine to the top of the feeder. "Finished already?" he asked.

16 "Yes, I am and just in time. I think I can hear those bugs eating my tomato buds right now. Dad, would you help me put this up in the pecan tree next to the garden?" asked Elena.

17 "Sure," Dad said.

18 Elena and Dad walked out the back door and headed to the pecan tree. They decided on a branch. Dad grabbed the ladder leaning against the fence and set it up under the low branch of the pecan tree. Elena climbed to the third step and tied the feeder to a slender limb. The feeder swung lazily in the soft breeze.

19 "Looks good!" said Dad. "Let's see if it helps."

20 Two weeks later Elena and Dad were standing next to the garden. Elena knelt down and looked carefully at one of the tomato plants.

21 "My tomato plants have never looked better," Elena said.

22 "You are right," Dad replied. "Now could I interest you in cleaning up your room and finishing your homework? Your mom will be home soon."

My Notes About What I Am Reading

(Category 2 – Figure 19 D – RS)

1 Which sentence from the story shows that Elena's problem in the story is solved?

   A "Get some birds to come to your garden," said Dad.
   B "My tomato plants have never looked better," Elena said.
   C "You mean go buy a couple of birds and keep them in a cage out in the garden?" asked Elena.
   D "Dad, would you help me put this up in the pecan tree next to the garden?" asked Elena.

(Category 3 – Figure 19 D – RS)

2 Why do the directions say to put rocks at the bottom of the bird feeder?

    A To hold the stick in place
    B To give the birds a place to sit
    C To help keep it still in the wind
    D To keep the birdseed from falling out

(Category 1 – 4 C – RS)

3 Which word from the passage means "all"?

    A Hour
    B Our
    C Hole
    D Whole

(Category 3 – 13 A – RS)

4 Which detail from the passage is important to the part titled "Bird Feeder"?

    A Fill the bottom of the carton with the birdseed.
    B "Mrs. Ruiz's plants next door always look so good."
    C "You mean go buy a couple of birds and keep them in a cage out in the garden?"
    D He went into the study and took a book off of one of the many shelves.

(Category 2 – 5 A – SS)

5   The theme of this story is

    A   keep plants safe.
    B   get rid of bugs.
    C   plant a garden.
    D   take care of your neighbor's garden.

(Category 3 – 13 C – RS)

6   The part from the passage titled "Bird Feeder" says that holes are put in the bottom of the bird feeder because

    A   birds need a way to get to the bird seed.
    B   water needs a way to leave the feeder.
    C   birds need a place to sit.
    D   people need a place to put twine to hang the feeder.

(Category 3 – 15 B – SS)

7   How is the small nail used with the bird feeder?

    A   To hang the feeder from a tree
    B   To put holes in the bottom of the feeder
    C   To serve as a perch
    D   To hold the string

Read the article "The Tallest Animal" before answering the questions below.

My Notes About What I Am Reading

ANIMAL ADVENTURES

Volume 4   **Animals of Africa**   October Issue

The Tallest Animal

1   The world's tallest animal towers above all others. Approaching 18 feet, these animals can weigh up to 2,600 pounds. Giraffes have very long necks. Reaching the tops of tall trees, giraffes are able to eat food most other animals are not able to get. A favorite food of the giraffe is the acacia leaf. These <u>moist</u> leaves help give the giraffe the water it needs to survive. Giraffes live in Africa where the weather is hot and dry.

2   The tongues of giraffes can grow to over 18 inches long. Their tongues are able to wrap around branches high in trees. Pulling on the branch, giraffes strip off the leaves. They do not chew the leaves very much at first. Instead, they keep them in the first of four stomachs. The giraffe brings the food back up its long neck to its mouth and chews on it some more. The giraffe swallows it again and the food goes through the other three stomachs.

3   Giraffes have very long legs. To get a drink of water, the giraffes have to put their front legs far apart. Then they can bend way down with their heads to reach the water. Strong, as well as long, the legs of the giraffes help them get away from enemies. Giraffes are fast. They can run up to 30 miles an hour over short distances. They can also use their <u>sturdy</u> legs to fight off any fierce enemies.

4   The hair on a giraffe is dark with light parts all around. Each giraffe has different spots. No two giraffes have the same spots. They help the giraffe blend in with the rest of the scenery. Enemies have a hard time spotting the giraffe because of the spots.

5   The tail of the giraffe helps keep bugs off of the giraffe's body. Long stringy hair hangs off of the end of the tail. Switching the tail

back and forth, the giraffe swats away flying and crawling pests from its body.

6 Giraffes have long necks. There are only seven bones in a giraffe's neck, just like other mammals. Strong muscles in the neck lift and move the giraffe's head. A giraffe can reach leaves at the top of tall trees. It also can use its head and neck to fight off other giraffes.

7 Giraffes usually live with other giraffes. A group of giraffes is called a troop. There may be from six to twelve giraffes in a troop. The animals move around looking for food in the early morning and late afternoon. They take time to rest during the hot middle part of the day.

8 A giraffe can live ten years or longer. It spends most of its life in one area. The giraffe is one of the world's most interesting animals.

My Notes About What I Am Reading

(Category 1 – 4 B – RS)

1 In paragraph 1, the word <u>moist</u> means

    A rough.
    B tall.
    C thin.
    D wet.

(Category 1 – 4 C – SS)

2 In paragraph 3, which word means the same as <u>sturdy</u>?

    A Fast
    B Fierce
    C Long
    D Strong

(Category 3 – 13 A – RS)

3 Paragraph 6 is important to the passage because it tells about

    A how a giraffe uses its neck.
    B the bones in a giraffe's body.
    C the tall trees that give a giraffe food.
    D how a giraffe fights its enemies.

(Category 3 – 16 – SS)

4   The picture is included in the passage to help the reader

    A identify the bones in a giraffe's neck.
    B learn how a giraffe gets food.
    C understand why giraffes live in groups.
    D know which time of day giraffes look for food.

(Category 3 – 13 A – RS)

5   Look at the chart below. It shows information from the article.

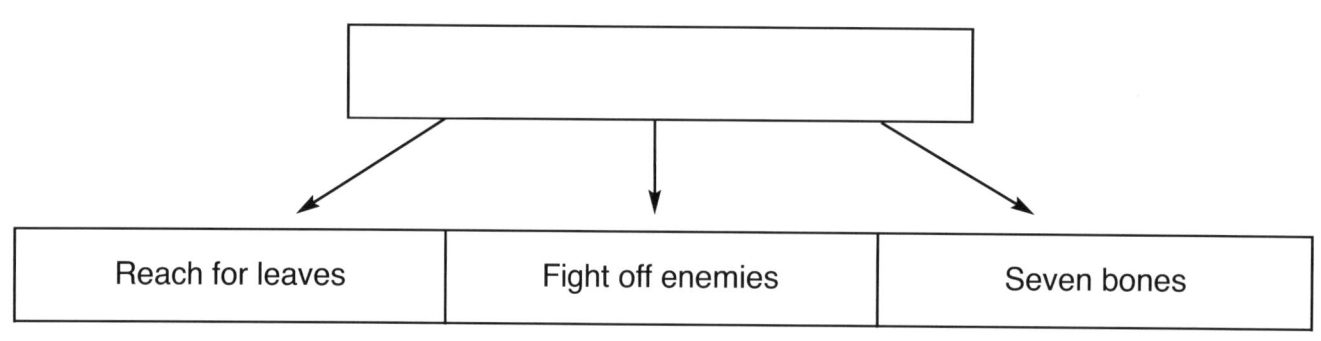

Reach for leaves	Fight off enemies	Seven bones

Which idea belongs in the empty box?

    A Head
    B Legs
    C Neck
    D Stomach

(Category 3 – Figure 19 D – RS)

6 From information provided in this article, the reader can tell that giraffes

    A have trouble keeping safe from enemies.
    B use their long necks to find food.
    C have several babies at one time.
    D move around to different living areas.

(Category 3 – Figure 19 E – RS)

7 Which is the best summary of the article?

    A Giraffes have long legs that help them run fast. Their long legs make it hard for giraffes to drink water. Giraffes have to stand with their legs far apart to be able to get water.
    B Giraffes are covered with spots. These spots help giraffes stay hidden in Africa. No two giraffes have the same spots.
    C Giraffes are tall animals that live in Africa. These creatures have four long legs, a long neck, and a long tongue to help them stay alive.
    D Giraffes like to eat leaves. The leaves are on branches of tall trees. Giraffes use their tongue to pull the leaves off of the branches.

Made in the USA
Middletown, DE
02 May 2024